UNDER THE BOARDWALK

UNDER THE
BOARDWALK

Norman Rosten

PRENTICE-HALL, INC., ENGLEWOOD CLIFFS, N.J.

Library of Congress Catalog Card Number: 68-26738

Printed in the United States of America · *T*

Prentice-Hall International, Inc., London
Prentice-Hall of Australia, Pty. Ltd., Sydney
Prentice-Hall of Canada, Ltd., Toronto
Prentice-Hall of India Private Ltd., New Delhi
Prentice-Hall of Japan, Inc., Tokyo

To my sisters
Dorothy,
Rose,
and
Sophie

UNDER THE BOARDWALK

~ 1 ~

At first, there was a beginning House, small, trim, and smelling of clean wood. Then, later, a middle House, a growing, never completed, diabolic House, perhaps even a laughing House. Finally, after I left, a remembered House, unreal, fading, small again.

The beginning House stood at the edge of the avenue set back from the sidewalk about twenty feet. It had a garden plot fronting the sidewalk. Slightly elevated, this was visible to all the other houses; in the spring a large blossoming rosebush gave the street a preposterous touch of elegance. The roses, in season, sent an aroma to the adjoining alleyways where windows would open to receive it. A half-flight of stone stairs began at the sidewalk and led up to an outside door with a transom of stained glass,

1

through a small vestibule, to the first landing. Inside, softened by opaque light, another flight of stairs curved to an upper floor. Each of the floors was divided into five rooms. It was officially designated by the Building Department as a two-family dwelling, and for a brief period remained true to its listing.

The middle House expanded. It filled up a large backyard, doubling the volume of the beginning House, doubling the rooms and stairways and windows, blocking the light with brick and steel, fusing the steel with the original wood structure. It invaded the front garden, obliterating the rosebush, the earth beneath, adding floor, walls, a roof, to become a store; then above that, walls and another roof to become another room, a room mysteriously unrecorded in the Building Department files. The middle House continued to grow without plan: rooms splitting off into other rooms, connecting pantries and baths jutting off into dwarfed nonarchitectural hallways, doors and closets seen and the next day covered over. A reshuffling of the bones, stairways, beams and ceilings, new pipes branching wildly away from the old, plaster patchwork, paint over wallpaper, wallpaper over paint, new walls for new tenants. And the tenants multiplied like insects on a wild plant.

The remembered House, derelict, leaning, odor of garbage and spice, aura of seawater, sweat clinging to the walls, and summer heat. Now endlessly receding, I see those rooms one inside the other like a Chinese box puzzle, each growing smaller, each box fitting within the other, each a replica of the other, and time secreted within . . .

"Rain," said the candystore man, standing in front of the house and dreaming of fair hot skies. "I smell rain like a curse."

"Rain rain go away," chanted my mother, poking her

head, puppet-like, out of the window, her laugh scatter-ing the pigeons.

My father, his inner wound throbbing, hating this time, this place, called from the street, "I hope it rains every day the rest of the summer." She chirped back, "Look up, look up at the sun and smile!" And her head pulled back inside.

And I in a still smaller box, not too far away, over-hearing all . . .

~ 2 ~

Come to Coney! The posters called, and everybody listened. And they came. On summer weekends a thousand people a minute spilled from the subway and trolley terminals and down Surf Avenue, some to the beach, some to the pools, sailors and girls waiting for evening, and the mystery of the place brocaded with lights and real stars.

Beyond the Amusement Park, over the rim of spires and pennants, just a block away, the mist was rising from the Atlantic, burning off under a high sun. It was going to be a good hot weekend. Let it rain Monday through Thursday, but Friday through Sunday let it stay clear and blue—this was the prayer of the merchant, and he prayed all summer long.

From the avenue right at the corner I could hear the early morning barkers trying out their voices: hurry hurry a nickel a nickel hurry a frank a root beer a nickel hurry potato chip fresh all fresh (fresh last week) and corn hot fresh (really warm and soggy) try a ride it's a dime take the little girl along she'll love to be kissed hurry hurry . . .

It was all starting up again, that long humid day of a million people, and nobody seemed to mind the lies and the sweat, or notice the rundown houses and streets full of the poor.

The High-Striker bell began to clang. I watched a guy proving his strength to his girl: slamming down the wooden mallet on the rubber pad which sent the slug shimmying up the tight wire, past Weakling past Weak Sister past 1500 past 2000 past Muscle Man and Sally and Lover Boy and Hercules all the way to the top: BONG! A box of candy, a Kewpie doll, souvenir! I flexed my boy's muscle and longed for the day when I could reach Hercules. BONG for the girl, O for a BONG!

Across the horizon, the empty ferris wheel towered, turning on its trial run. The outside gondolas kept an easy balance, while inside the wheel a series of looped over-head tracks allowed other gondolas to drop and swing in tight arcs, rocking until they gently came to rest. At night, a thousand, maybe ten thousand electric bulbs framed the wheel, and on a clear night, when the lights turned, it was as if the nearby stars were turning along with them, you couldn't be sure.

The rides were warming up. Every two or three minutes, a string of cars whooshed and clanked around the curve of the roller coaster, to disappear down the spidery tracks and drop into a dip of great delight before it sped upward again. Soon the screams of girls would be heard on the turns and drops, rising above the clatter of the cars. I knew the girls were locked in their seats and couldn't escape, and on the drops they would freeze and scream, and when you pulled them close they were too busy screaming to fight back if you held their breasts or slid a hand under their dress. I heard all kinds of stories about what went on down those drops but maybe they were lies, too.

You couldn't tell what was real in a place like this. Whenever you thought something was real, the music of a calliope would start up. It was one of the problems in living here. Maybe that's what the signs meant: Come to Coney! Come to the land where you can't tell what's real! Hurry hurry . . .

Each morning as the sun's heat slowly glazed the streets, the garbage truck came by. Its side panels were about six feet high, forming an open box. Inside, the garbage man labored in dungarees, high boots, and a T-shirt. A handkerchief was tightly bound across his forehead, his hands covered with heavy asbestos gloves. The truck moved slowly along, as two other men dragged or rolled the refuse-laden cans from the curb into the street. With a rhythmic grunt-and-lift, together they heaved the can to the lip of the panel, where the man inside seized it, shifted it to his hip, and in a continuing movement spilled the contents into the boxed area. Then, without a pause, he flipped the empty can over the side where waiting hands received it, spinning it to the curb while a partner began rolling another loaded can toward the truck. Together, they repeated their lifting maneuver with a loud *Ho,* while the driver crept along at a slow steady pace.

By the time it reached our house, the truck was almost full, the mounds piled high in the corners. A foul odor, like a haze, hung over it. The man, standing higher now in the center, waist-deep in garbage, was covered with sweat while around his head an army of black flies buzzed.

6

Large, heavy-winged, swarming above the stench, descending in waves, they settled on his arms as though to devour him whole, but the garbage man kept to his rhythm, taking the can, emptying it, tossing it back over the side. When finally the truck passed our house, a gang of waiting boys flung apple rinds, chicken bones, even bottles into it, yelling at the figure balanced on the pile.

"Hey, stinky, here's more garbage!"

"Phew, you stink!"

"Get a horse!"

Someone always had balls of dried horse dung ready, and tossed them like grenades, taunting the man who said nothing, who moved his glistening arms black with flies, until the truck reached the avenue.

I followed. It was time to do my work.

My job at this prenoon hour was to hawk bathers for the locker establishment in our house. In the summer season, we rented locker space to as many people we could squeeze into it. There were all kinds of "clubs," for example, ten boys and girls, sharing one room on weekends. My mother enjoyed the confusion. She would even allow part of our own apartment to be used if the demand was great. On some weekends we rented the garage (which was really a storeroom). One summer I slept in the hallway on a small folding-cot I carried around most of the time so I'd be sure of having something to lie on. On a holiday, relatives always came to visit and I'd sleep on the beach or under the boardwalk. It was like a camping trip without going anywhere.

Our regular bath lockers (built in our basement because nothing much was going on in that empty basement and my mother liked to have things going on everywhere) could squeeze in over fifty people. Not that there were fifty lockers. My mother had a system of renting each locker several times a day, and hanging the clothes in a storeroom, so that at the end of the day nobody was sure whom he might find dressing in his locker. I remember a lot of screaming and giggling but nobody complained. My mother's place was always a sellout.

I didn't like my job, being thrust this way into a world of strangers, having to call out: *Lockers twenty-five cents hot and cold showers no waiting.* There was always waiting, and I hated to call out lies, but nobody seemed to mind. On a good morning I'd haul in maybe twenty-five and many more would come by themselves.

The avenue was full of suckers that morning, and I got about fifteen customers in less than an hour. I had all sorts of tricks such as grabbing the duffle bag while giving my pitch or if it was a young couple I'd speak my lines to the girl so that the boy would show he could make up his mind and it was easier to say yes. Most people liked yes better than no. My mother taught me these tricks, she made them up one every minute.

My work completed early, I decided to take a swim. I was already in my swim trunks. I raced barefoot over the hot pavement toward the beach a block away, stopping to cool my feet in patches of tree shade.

I had to dash under the boardwalk to get to the beach. Midway under it, I paused to catch my breath. A chill of apprehension touched me with the sudden cold air. A fetid odor rose up from the sand: it seemed to come from a subterranean source, born of sewage seeping in from the ocean and absorbed in the deepest layers of earth.

In this place of half light, sunlight flaked down through the boards, a pattern of gold running straight, then diagonally, then straight again. I chased the filtered light until it unraveled and ended at the concrete pillars. I played games with it: cutting it up, throwing sand on it, catching it in the air with my open mouth, or letting it tremble on my eyelids. Tired of that, I zigzagged be-

8

tween the pillars, my heart pounding, looking up through the thin spacings between the boards in search of ladies who left their underwear home, an Indian stalking his prey.

Under the boardwalk, for miles, stretched a fringe of corrugated metal and wire fence, entrances to locker houses, frayed billboards, rotting wood, and decayed boats alive with rats and mongrel dogs. Some of the Steeplechase rides skirted the area. You could hear, if you were close to the fence, the rustle of water where the gondola glided through the Tunnel of Love. Nearby, in the shadows, men and women loitered, silent, some holding hands, some clinging to each other, a man pressing a girl against the concrete pillar, a girl combing a man's hair, others watching, silent, waiting.

It was spooky under here. I leaped again into the blinding sun where the sand blazed at my feet and the edge of water rose and fell just a little ways ahead. I was glad to be out in the light again. I skipped over legs, arms, and heads, gathering myself for the plunge. The breakers roared in my ears. Skinny, my soul half-formed, I dived over a rim of foam and under the heaving wall of water.

The coolness enfolded me. My lungs ballooned with air. I became a fish, my glazed eyes open to the green world below. I saw glistening legs of swimmers, slow-motion thrashing legs, erotic and muffled in the sea-green meadow. How my heart hungered! I was a fish nibbling at weeds, nudging at limbs, swimming round and round those languorous girls like the ones in the bathing suit ads with their lips smiling and their legs together like fins.

Down I propelled to a colder level. In my ears boomed the faraway hiss of surf—all the way from Europe or Africa! I had no pain or cares, and overhead I knew the world waited with its flowering sun. I was far from my

9

house and my mother's caution. In an instant, I saw my drowning death, the funeral route, my face unsmiling in the open casket. My mother weeping, my father stunned, cousins and uncles and aunts in dreadful black veils, all rushed past my eyes. They'd miss me, they'd suffer. O this power I had!

My feet kicked bottom sand. My lungs tired. I turned my stroke upward, the green became lighter, and I broke into sunlight, gasping for air. I hung onto the rope, breathing hard. The shore seemed to retreat, grow small, the landscape beyond the boardwalk—ferris wheel, parachute drop, loop-the-loop, Steeplechase—becoming a child's cutout.

With short quick strokes I swam to the shore, edging past a grapefruit rind that rode the wave with the ease of a yellow boat.

By now, at noon, the beach was almost filled. Of course, you never can fill up a beach, the whole idea of a beach is that no matter how crowded it gets you can always squeeze another thousand people in. People were stepping over other people, jumping over other people, calling or staring down at other people. Through this jumbled mass, more other people were maneuvering toward the water which you couldn't see because of the density of the crowd. Voices and sounds merged to a hum, the buzzing of an immense hive.

I lay face down on the sand, my bones stretching in the heat, my head turned slightly in the crook of my arm where, as through a keyhole, I could steal forbidden glimpses of this world. Red, white, blue, green, yellow umbrellas. A sudden kiss, a breast revealed, a hand at rest upon a thigh, a gently stroking motion. I watched and dreamed with eyes open.

Then, filtering through the hum, through the haze, a faint sound drifted to my ears. At first I thought it was someone singing. As the sound came closer, I recognized the chant of the pretzel man.

He moved carefully through the sun-baked sand, head bent forward, wearing sneakers, loose trousers, faded sport shirt, and a round straw skullcap. He was an old man, his skin weathered by sun and wind. Supported by rope which cut into his shoulders, a large basket of pretzels hung at his hip. The pretzels were mounted on sticks jutting vertically from the basket. Slowly, accurately, he stepped between the people sprawled everywhere, calling *Pretzels ten cents fresh pretzels.*

Close by, he set the basket on the sand. He wiped the sweat from his face, groaning softly. Then he sat down, took off his sneakers and shook the sand out, thoughtfully, one sneaker at a time. He looked up at the sky. He reached for a small water flask from his pocket and drank. A group of kids rushed by, their heels kicking sand against the basket, and he yelled after them, "Hey, hey, watch out! Gangsters!"

I counted the pretzels on the sticks. I counted at least twenty-five. My mouth hungered. Maybe he'd drop one? A woman alongside of me turned toward him. "How much the pretzels?"

"Ten cents."

"For one?"

"Naturally. Would it be ten cents a dozen?"

"And three?"

"Thirty cents, lady."

"I saw three for a quarter on the boardwalk."

"On the beach it's ten cents."

"At the subway station it's even five cents."

"Go to the station then, if you please."

"Give me one," said the woman.

The pretzel man folded back the white cloth which covered part of the basket, removed one pretzel from the stick, and replaced the cloth. He accepted a coin, reached into his pocket, and made change.

The woman asked, "These are fresh?"

He answered firmly. "Baked fresh this morning."

My mouth was watering. I wondered, if he'd turn his back for a moment, whether I'd have the courage to slip a pretzel off the stick. He would hardly miss one pretzel. He suddenly stiffened and gave a little cry. My eyes followed his gaze. Coming down from the boardwalk stairs, at a slight trot, a policeman moved toward him. He swung the basket to his shoulder and started quickly toward the water.

As he passed me, I reached up and neatly picked a pretzel off the stick and, with the same motion, slid it under my shirt. I fell back to the sand. It was so easy I wanted to laugh—and practically in front of the cop, too! The pretzel smelled good, the pungent dough, the salt. But I wouldn't eat it right away. I wanted to see what would happen first.

I got up and followed the policeman. Onlookers were converging toward him from all directions, anticipating an arrest or, better still, a brawl. The old man had broken into a run, the basket swinging perilously at his side. As he ran, he kicked off his sneakers, tossed away his shirt and, at the water's edge, setting the basket carefully down, he got out of his trousers. He wore swimming trunks underneath. With a mute look at the amused spectators, he plunged into the water, still wearing the straw skullcap, and swam out to the rope.

The policeman came up to the shore, waving his nightstick. "Come out, you!"

The pretzel man, puffing at the rope, bobbing up and down with the mild waves, called back, "What for?"

"I warned you yesterday to get off the beach."

"So I forgot."

"If I catch you around again, y'hear, I'll give you a summons."

"Ha, ha," the old man laughed wildly, adjusting his hat.

The crowd laughed. The policeman flicked his club impatiently. The pretzel man called out, "Come in here and give me a summons, ha, ha!" The policeman pointed at him with his nightstick, shouting, "Keep off the beach. Last warning!" He started to walk away. The voice from the water called after him, "It's against the law to eat, is that right? I have to make a living!" He pulled himself along the rope toward the shore, his voice shrill, "I have to make a living, tell that to the captain. Go put crooks in jail, I'm not a crook. I have a family, a sick wife . . ."

The policeman disappeared. Two kids ran up from nowhere, snatched pretzels off the stick, and darted away. The crowd laughed. The old man scrambled out of the water. He waved to the cop, "Catch them, catch the little gangsters!" He started chasing the kids, but soon gave up. He came back to the basket, reached for his trousers and put them on over his dripping trunks; he found his shirt and his sneakers. He lifted the basket to his shoulder and peered into the crowd. "Come out, you little crooks! I know you're hiding!"

Several youths scooped up handfuls of sand and ran by with Indian whoops, tossing the sand over the pretzels. The old man kicked at them savagely. "Gangsters!" he shouted. Tears sprang to his eyes. He blew the sand from the pretzels, shifted the weight of the basket more evenly on his shoulders, and started off.

I followed him along the beach. I was hungry, but now I couldn't eat the stolen pretzel. The old man kept a wary eye ahead and behind, stopping often to scan the beach for any sign of the law. I stopped when he did, jogged after him when he started up again. I figured if I got up close, I could slip the pretzel back on the stick. I closed in on him. As he was making a sale, I edged toward the basket, at the same time holding the pretzel ready. Suddenly he looked up and saw me. His body stiffened. "Here's one of them! You want to steal more?" And he lunged at me. I stepped back, and easily vanished in the crowd. I heard his voice. "Gangster, let me catch you, if I catch you . . . Where is he?"

I lay on the sand, breathing heavily. Soon he was calling again, going off, *Pretzels fresh a dime fresh every time*. I rose, and ran a wide circle ahead of him, then dropped to the sand, waiting for him to pass. The pretzel, heated by my body, grew sticky under my shirt. This time I wouldn't try to get it on the stick, but just run by and toss it into the basket.

Through a lattice of sprawled and passing figures, I watched him approach. He was coming in a straight line, but as he neared me he turned off in answer to a customer's shout. I figured this was a good time to do it.

I got up again, pressed toward him, swallowing, because I was hungry now, real hungry, and it was crazy not to eat the pretzel, but I couldn't eat it, I knew that, and wanted to get it out of my hands as soon as possible. I broke into a trot and swerved so that I would cut directly across his path.

I had just reached him, when he saw me again. His eyes lit up with surprise. He swung his arm, as if to strike me, and swung the basket behind him so I couldn't toss the pretzel into it. I continued my run past him and stopped helplessly a little way off.

"I'll catch you, wait!"

"Take your lousy pretzel," I yelled. "I don't want it."

"You want to steal, heh?"

"Listen, I don't want it. Here, take it." I held out the pretzel, looking very foolish with all the people watching, but all he did was to shout at me and curse me, so I moved off and disappeared again into the crowd. I watched him pass me, getting smaller and smaller until he was lost in the swirling hive, the sun-drenched day. The pretzel was now soggy from my sweat. I took one bite, then hurled it into the water.

I ran back to the house. I wanted to get the pretzel man out of my mind. Passing the locker room, I stuck my head into the shower, and the ladies clucked and screamed like a bunch of chickens.

I felt better already.

~3~

My grandmother was totally blind and loved conversation, except she did all the talking, which created a problem for her children, as well as grandchildren, nieces and nephews, and anyone else who happened to wander into her range. She sat on a chair outside the house and, with the sharp hearing of a bird, pounced upon any sound. "Who's there? I know you're there! Is it Sam, Jimmy, Michael, Irving?" She cocked her head, listened, and if the person addressed attempted to sneak off, she would level a barrage of curses: "Come back, you little monster! Where are you going? My daughter's own son, won't you come and sit a while with your grandmother and talk to her? Little monsters, all of you. God who sees all, see crazy Irving and Sam who won't as much as say good morning to me. Curse them, send them to hell!"

Then, a moment later, she would murmur sweetly, "I've lived. I can't complain. I've lived to be eighty at least. I have decent sons and daughters keeping the faith in a land of Christians, and my grandchildren, bless them, growing up . . . why should I complain, dear God?"

And she rarely did complain. But the hours were long and lonesome, and her need to talk was desperate. My mother was too busy with chores to spend more than a few fleeting minutes a day with her; the neighbors had long ago tired of the old lady's relentless monologues and stayed clear of her. Inside the house, she kept talking to herself so loudly it interfered with homework or listening to the radio. She had been living with us for the past year, since Grandfather could no longer care for her. He stayed on in his own place a block away and came by often to visit. I think he liked living by himself. My father grumbled about the whole situation and frequently shouted at her, whereupon she spun out a series of curses that I didn't understand but felt the wind of as they hurled across the room.

My mother, anxious to keep peace in the family (though enjoying the brisk disorder of family battles), called a meeting of her brothers to decide about Grandmother. They arrived, everyone sat and drank tea and debated the problem.

I liked my uncles. They always gave me pennies, sometimes a nickel, and they joked a lot. Uncle Morty told me it didn't matter if I was bad in school, as long as I smiled. "All the world loves a smile," he said. "Now smile. Good. Bigger. That's good!"

"I refuse to take her," summed up Uncle Ralph, puffing on a cigar. "I have enough problems." And he did, you could tell by the way he puffed.

"I also refuse," said Uncle Morty, the inventor who never invented anything. "It's true, she's our mother. But she's too old. Send her to a home, it's the kindest thing."

"A home, that's the place," echoed Uncle Ezra picking his teeth with a golden toothpick which he showed at every visit.

My mother shook her head. "Never will I send my own mother to a strange place with nobody to talk to."

"She can talk to herself," suggested Uncle Morty with a smirk. "She's doing it now."

"And don't *you* ever do it?" my mother snapped.

"He's been talking to himself all his life," exclaimed Uncle Ralph, laughing like a hyena and choking on his cigar.

Uncle Ezra got up to leave. "How long can she live, anyway?"

"If the Old One would go, she'd hurry maybe," said Uncle Ralph. The Old One was my grandfather. They were sitting around, imagine, hoping my grandfather would die, and my grandmother too! My ears burned at what I heard—except for my mother, she didn't feel the way her brothers did. But she didn't seem to be angry enough at them for saying what they said. It was hard to figure out.

Finally the meeting ended. Grandmother was staying with us because nobody knew what to do about the problem.

She caught me outside more than anyone else. She seemed to smell me coming up the alleyway where she sat taking the sun. "Who's there? It's you! Don't run away!"

"I'm not running away, Grandma," I said, ashamed that she could read my thoughts.

"So, sit down, we'll talk." She heard me groan. "What did you say?"

"I got homework, Grandma."

"You haven't any homework in the summer. You're

18

a little liar. Did your mother give you poison to put in my tea?"

I watched her thin lips open and close like a wax dummy fortune-teller in the penny arcade. Her eyes were usually closed, and a watery substance trickled down from them onto her dress. Thin and bent, she leaned forward in the chair, working her fingers nervously. I was terrified by her skin: cracked, wrinkled, spotted with red. Like a matted nest, her white hair, rarely washed, gave out a weak nauseating odor. When she gripped my hand or my arm, I couldn't get away for an hour. And she talked and talked. She had to reach out and touch you when she talked; it was her way of knowing you were actually there, she wouldn't trust you otherwise.

". . . and you'll grow up, but what will become of you in the land of *goyim*? I spit when I think of them." And she spat.

"Cut it out, Grandma. That's no way to talk."

"I speak the truth."

"If you're gonna spit every time you see a Christian, you'll just die spitting, you won't have any spit left."

She wet her lips. "There aren't so many. How many can they be?"

"There are millions, Grandma," I said sullenly. I hated to discuss this with her.

"Where? Where are there millions?"

"Right in the city. In Brooklyn, the Bronx, everywhere. We're just a minority."

"But they won't destroy us!"

"Gee, Grandma, they don't want to destroy us. I go to school with all sorts of kids, and Negroes too—"

"The worst! Black Christians!" And she spat.

"They're my friends. I just think you're wrong to sit here hating people."

She stared at me, sightless, silent, then shook her head

19

from side to side, and a little wordless lullaby came from her lips. Then she covered her mouth with her hands, as if to prevent herself from speaking a blasphemy. I saw her walled in by a profound and overwhelming ignorance, and I loved her out of pity. I listened, and often answered her, but she did not need or really want answers; she wanted a living person beside her, to hear her old tales a hundred times told within her dark self, to feel the ashes of her remembered life stirring. And I sat with her clawlike hand biting into my arm until she fell asleep. Then my mother would motion me inside the house, and kiss me. "You're a good boy, and God will reward you." She went on, "Your grandmother is a terrible problem. It breaks my heart just to see her talking to herself day after day."

In time the old lady became more troublesome. She called out and seized strangers by the arm. One neighbor complained, "The old lady is crazy, she should be locked up." To which my mother replied, "She may *look* crazy, my dear, but you *are* crazy!" We made a lot of enemies on our street.

Finally, one day, the neighbor brought a policeman around to prove that my grandmother was crazy and should be taken away.

"How can I tell?" said the cop uneasily, staring at my grandmother, as neighbors circled around.

"Listen to her talk!" screamed the neighbor.

"Listen to *you* talk!" shouted my mother.

The cop clamped his nightstick. "I dunno."

"Who's there?" asked Grandmother. "Is it you, Irving, you monster? Come, sit down, I have a story."

"This ain't my department," said the cop, backing off.

"That woman isn't fit to sit here on the sidewalk and scare little children!" shouted the neighbor.

20

"Listen to this old lady, Officer," my mother persuaded. "Sit down. Judge for yourself. I'll get you a cold drink." She ran inside and returned with some iced lemonade, gently sat the wondering policeman in the chair next to Grandmother and waited. The group of neighbors closed in.

Grandmother reached out her hand and felt the strange fabric of the policeman's jacket. "Who is it? Ah, a stranger! Someone who is kind, who has a gentle heart to spend time with a blind old lady. What's your name? All right, we don't need a name today. As long as you're not a *goy*."

The policeman met the titter of the crowd with a smile, leaned back in the chair, and sipped at the lemonade.

"Long ago," my grandmother began, "when I came to this country as a little girl, I remember I had a blue dress. My own mother, bless her, made that dress for me with her own hands . . ." On and on about the dress, up to how she got married. Boy, I thought she'd never stop.

The neighbors drifted away, except for the complainer, who waited until Grandmother let her hand relax on the policeman's arm. He rose, straightening his jacket.

"She should be taken away to a bughouse," said the red-faced neighbor.

The policeman shook his head. "It's not my department," he said walking off.

The neighbor ran after him, "She scares little children!" But the policeman kept on walking.

We kept running out of listeners for Grandmother. My sister refused and even wept when forced to keep her company. I started getting into arguments with her, so that she didn't want me near. My mother found a drunken sailor to sit there and listen, but he started yelling at Grandmother, and she spat at him. The problem was getting more unsolved every day.

Then, one day, my mother had a special look in her eye. She called me over and said, "I have an idea. Go catch me a dog." I knew my mother got all kinds of ideas, but this sounded craziest of all. I stared at her. "A dog," she repeated.

"What for?"

"First catch him, then I'll tell you. There are lots of nice dogs running around on the avenue. Find one that's gentle and bring him here." I was too curious to refuse.

Armed with a rope, I scouted around and finally spotted a large but tame-looking mongrel. The minute I came up to him, he began wagging his tail and licking my hand. He looked gentle. I slipped the rope around his neck and he trotted after me happily.

My mother embraced me when she saw the dog. "He's just right. God will reward you." Before I could ask one question, she went inside and brought out a large bowl of leftover food. The dog sniffed and followed her. She led him to the garage in back of the house where Grandmother was sitting. We had moved her away from the front of the house because she was talking too loud.

"Who's there?" asked Grandmother. "If it's him, my grandson, that monster, I don't want him!"

My mother said, "It's only me." She led the dog next to Grandmother, tied him to a chair, set the bowl of food before him, and waited to one side.

"Who's there?" repeated Grandmother, her hand reaching out. Her fingers touched the dog and drew back. He licked her hand. He then started crunching the bowl of food. "A dog? Not a dog." Her voice rose. "You monster daughter, you accursed of God, a dog!" Then, softly, "Where are you, little dog?" Her hand found his back, and she stroked him. He uttered a grateful little bark. The bark delighted Grandmother. "Oh, you sweet little dog. Eat. I hear you eating. What a nice tail you have. A good brave little dog. You'll sit next to me and I'll tell you a story."

It was a stroke of genius. The dog sat next to Grandmother, acknowledging her with little barks, wagging his tail happily as her hand stroked his head. She talked on and on, making her more dramatic points with sudden squeezings of his tail, which changed his bark to a yelp, but she went on with her rambling narrative. "Are you still here, dear little thing? Of course, you're tied up, but you like it here, don't you? Later I'll tell you about my husband. He's a rascal. He's a dog, do you hear me, dog?" And she laughed. "He chased women all the time, that dog. You understand what I mean, eh?" The dog, half-asleep, responded to her hand with a whimper. Soon she too leaned to the arm of the chair and was asleep.

I watched Grandmother asleep and I wondered how I would feel when she died. Because she would have to die soon, she was just too old to go on, I mean not only blind but smelly and a little loco in the head.

Good-bye, Grandmother! I bet you'll be happy to die. You always spoke of God, and I know how badly you want to see Him, you're so sure He's there, waiting, and I hope He is there so you won't be disappointed. If He exists He should absolutely meet you when you get There. All the time you gave to Him, all those prayers, the religious holidays—if He doesn't meet you and kiss you, He's a rat!

Good-bye! I wonder if I'll kiss you when you become dead. Will I be scared? You're so ugly, but I remember how you once sang to me when I was falling asleep with a fever, and your voice was soft and kind, and you became young but I kept my eyes closed because I knew you were sitting next to my bed as ugly as a rhino in a zoo. Yet your voice was love . . .

I bent over her as she slept. I saw the knotted hands on her lap. I heard her slow uncertain breathing. She was so near the end of everything.

I kissed her cheek, almost overcome by the odor of her matted white hair. She called out in her sleep, "Who's there? Little monster! Did you come to poison me?"

Then I hated her more than ever. "Drop dead, you old witch!" I yelled. The dog awoke and began to bark. My mother came out of the house and shook her head, pretending to be horrified.

∽ 4 ∽

It was the time of the Holidays, the weather bringing a hint of summer. The grownups took it very seriously. I had to do the same. You can't laugh at something when everyone else around you believes in it. Everybody acted strangely during this period, they cried a little then laughed so hard you didn't know what to believe. But the whole thing, the Holiday itself, Passover, was serious I guess. After all, you couldn't celebrate all that religion and history just for fun. The children of ancient Israel being chased out of Egypt by this Pharaoh after suffering all kinds of plagues, and then Moses leading them into the wilderness—if that isn't serious I don't know what is.

And there was my grandfather. I wanted to be serious just for him. On the Holidays I always tried to behave as best I could, to make him happy. He was a little scary, my grandfather, with his large face and heavy beard and his eyes looking right into you. But I knew he was kind. He liked me even though I had disappointed him by not going to religious school. I went for a while, but the long hours at a desk with a language I could never grasp soon made me ill. I complained of headaches. My mother said I was working too hard. But it was my father who decided that I go to public school only. I felt better.

Often, on the Sabbath eve, I watched my grandfather give the blessings over food. He recited them with his eyes closed, like he had a secret he didn't want to share. On the Holidays, the prayers got worse, they didn't stop for days, a whole week, they were all about suffering and miracles. God and the prophets were running around all the time in those early times. You didn't know what to believe.

I discussed the whole thing with my friend Jimmy Berkowitz. "Aah, it's all fairy tales, all that stuff," commented Jimmy with derision. "Like Moses lifting his arm and telling the Red Sea to move back so they could cross over on dry land. You believe that?"

"Well, it could happen," I said.

"The sea could divide in *half,* you believe it?"

"If it was a miracle," I insisted. "Things like that are miracles, so you gotta believe." I never knew how to answer him.

He leered at me. "C'mon, we'll go to the ocean right now and I'll lift my arm and holler 'Go back, water, I wanna cross over to New Jersey.' What do you think would happen? Right—nuthin'."

"Yeah, but if it was like a great emergency, and you were a leader—" I persisted.

"That's for the birds!" he cut in. "You go to the synagogue on the Holy Days?"

26

"Sometimes."

"Don't your parents go?"

"Only my grandparents. My mother, sometimes. My father, never. He says it's all a fake, God is a fake."

Jimmy whistled in admiration. "Boy, I hate to think what'll happen to your old man if God is really up there waiting for him. Poom! One look and he's the Invisible Man!" He laughed and slapped his head and hopped on one leg pretending to shake water out of his ear.

I was alarmed at the thought of God punishing my father or making him invisible. "God would never do that. He forgives you if you mean well."

Jimmy was relentless. "Your old man is gonna fry like a hot dog at Nathan's, ho, ho!" And he ran off, leaving me with a hollow twinge near my heart. I felt a thrill of identification with my father. Imagine, to call God a fake, that was bravery! My father was brave, no matter what anyone could say about him. I saw my father facing God, and God would say: I exist and you have made a terrible mistake and you will pay the penalty, and my father would look right back at Him and say: I am ready, and God would say: Who else didn't believe in me? Did your son believe? (I shivered, waiting his reply.) And he said: Yes, he believes.

My father lied to save me! But if it was a lie, God would know (God Almighty, All-Seeing, All-Knowing), and He might strike me down. Maybe on the Passover Holiday He was testing me, to see what I would do. I bet He didn't like me listening to Jimmy. I got a cold sweat thinking about it.

My uncles didn't believe in God, I could tell, but my aunts did, and my grandfather most of all. Sometimes I got the idea he thought *he* was God, I mean the way he acted, very slow and important and wise, the way he lifted his arm when he asked for a glass of water (Moses

27

lifting his arm to the Red Sea!) or how he smoothed his beard so carefully. Well, if he didn't think he was God, I bet he thought he was pretty close. He prayed like he was real close, like God was watching him personally, breathing down his neck almost.

Passover night arrived. The relatives filled up all the places around the table, joking and teasing, while Grandfather looked over the assemblage like a big rough-combed rooster counting his family. The Holiday had lots of funny dishes and prayers. There was one big dish with bitter herbs and vegetables, floating in salt water, also a combination of nuts, apples, raisins, a roasted lamb bone, and a roasted egg. Also, four cups of wine were to be drunk by every member of the family seated around the table. Not to mention having to listen to the stories and songs all about being chased out of Egypt, mixed with prayers. Whenever my sister and cousins giggled or grew restless, Grandfather's eyes (Dracula's eyes!) would fix us with a relentless gaze that froze us to attention. It was hard to listen and not understand. I liked the singsong parts, but after a while I got sleepy and had to fight to keep awake.

In front of each place on the table was a wineglass filled with wine. At certain times in the ceremony, the grownups would lift their glasses and take a swallow. But there was one glass that held my attention. It was the special glass no one lifted. That glass, they told me, was reserved for the angel Elijah. The door to the room remained slightly ajar for Elijah to enter if he so wished, and to be refreshed by the wine. A messenger of God, who could come as a guest. An angel to visit us! What if he chose to visit us this night, to come to this house of all the houses in the world? The idea of a real angel entering the room made me giddy. Was it possible? Did they believe it, or was it a game? Could an angel come

28

in through the small opening of the door? I guess it could squeeze through sideways, or maybe it floated through like smoke—did anyone ever *see* an angel? Suppose it lifted the glass—but that would be impossible. It probably just bent down and took a sip. How much could an angel sip? Could an angel get drunk, I wondered?

All these questions raced around in my head along with the murmuring prayers. I once wanted to ask my grandfather some of these questions, but I was afraid he'd become angry. You had to be careful of what you asked an old religious man, especially if he gave you a nickel sometimes.

Grandfather was booming along with the ceremony. I tried to follow him in the little book which had the Jewish letters running from right to left on one half of the page, and the English translation going from left to right on the other half. I was skipping lots of words, but I knew enough to keep track of him.

". . . our God, King of the Universe, who hast kept us alive, and hast maintained us, and hast enabled us to reach this time . . ." Then washing hands. Then dipping greens in salt water. "Blessed art thou, Lord, our God, King of the Universe, who dost create the fruit of the soil . . ." Then breaking half of the matzah and lifting the ceremonial plate. "This is the poor bread which our fathers ate in the land of Egypt. Let anyone who is hungry, come in and eat; let anyone who is needy, come in and make Passover. This year we are here; next year we shall be in the land of Israel. This year we are slaves; next year we shall be freemen."

Then he turned to me, at the same time removing the ceremonial plate and pouring a second cup. I was the youngest, and I had to do this next thing, which was called The Four Questions. I had it memorized. "Why is this night different from all other nights? On all other nights, we eat leavened bread and matzah; on this night, we eat only matzah. On all other nights, we eat all kinds of herbs; on this night, we eat mainly bitters. On all other nights, we do not dip even once; on this night, we dip twice . . ." I was going along great. My grandfather—I could see him out of the corner of my eye—looked pleased. (Maybe he'd give me a dime before he left!)

Then it happened. I saw it happening. The angel entered the room. Elijah, thin and pale, looking at no one, glided in, floated in, and stopped. He wore clothes, but not like any clothes I could recognize, more like a silky cloak that ruffled in the breeze. But there was no breeze —we were in a room! His face turned toward me but he did not see me. It was a face of eager and luminous beauty, a light seemed to come from within it and radiated outward. All the while his clothes stirred as though by a delicate wind. He slowly moved toward the table where the solitary untouched wineglass waited. He saw the glass and bent forward, leaning down . . .

I shouted, "The angel. I see the angel!"

They stared at me, my grandfather, grandmother, father, mother, sister, uncles, aunts, and cousins. Their faces swayed before me.

"What's with you?" my grandfather spoke hoarsely.

"The angel. Right next to you!"

"Why are you interrupting?" he sputtered. "Be quiet or leave the room."

The angel seemed like a mist before my eyes. His lips were now touching the rim of the wineglass.

"Look," I whispered, and pointed.

Nobody moved. They thought I was crazy. I heard my mother's reassuring but urgent voice. "What is it? What do you see?"

"The angel," I moaned. "Drinking the wine."

My grandfather exploded. "Get the boy out of here.

What angel? What are you talking about? You don't see an angel. Only God can see one!"

"I see him. I see him!" I screamed.

My mother was alarmed and came over to me, putting her arm around my shoulder. Now my father rose from his chair in a sudden movement. "The boy has a fever. And why? I will tell you why." He turned and spoke directly to my grandfather. "Because you have stuffed his head with nonsense, with foolish stories, with God and angels and miracles. Every month it's something else, another holiday, another miracle of the Jews. Enough miracles!" His face was flushed, his fingers red from gripping the table. "This is America. Nobody believes in such stories anymore."

Grandfather roared back. "I believe. That is enough!"

"Believe by yourself, then!"

"God's wrath will strike you one day. You have violated the Holy Days. You have labored on these days—"

My father slammed the table. "I will do what I please. And you be careful or you won't be allowed inside this house, do you hear me?"

My mother started to cry. Uncle Ezra reached for a radish and tipped over his wineglass. My aunts and cousins sat rigidly in their chairs. Uncle Morty flung down his napkin. "It's a bughouse here!" My grandmother shouted, "What's happening? Why don't we sing?"

All this must have scared the angel, because he got smaller and smaller and finally vanished.

"He's going away," I wailed softly.

"Be quiet," said my father grimly. "Not another word from you. Go to your room." Then, to Grandfather, "Finish this business tonight, but without me, and without the boy. And tomorrow night, please, pray somewhere else."

My mother wept openly, loudly, despairingly. My

father turned to the others. "Let her cry. The father sings, the daughter cries. Each has a trick." He passed me at the door where I had lingered. "Go to bed," he said in an iron voice and vanished.

My grandfather hurled a final thunderbolt at his back. "Satan!" he hissed. And then, to me, quivering, "An angel, hah! If it was given to anyone to see this angel, then it would be me. Is that clear? And another thing, my little dreamer, He would not send His angel to this house of anti-God!"

"Then why do you keep the wineglass ready?" I pleaded. They were all silent now, watching.

"Why? It's the ceremony."

"Then it's not true?"

"Of course it's true," he snapped. "A thing does not have to happen to be true. To see a thing doesn't prove anything. *Belief* is what proves."

He was confusing me again, like all the grownups. "Well, I saw it!" I shot back at him and ran out. I heard behind me the sudden buzz of talk, my aunts now getting into the act, and above the voices flying across the air behind me, the sound of my mother's weeping followed until I reached my room and shut the door. I was sad, and leaned against the window where my eye caught a cluster of stars far away over the rooftop, millions of miles away. Was God up there, really watching everybody? The stars seemed to tremble, as if they wanted to speak.

It was hours later when my grandfather stopped in to say good night. I didn't know what to say and was glad when he spoke first. "Are you all right, boy?" he asked gently.

"Yes, Grandpa."

"Such noise on a holiday I don't enjoy," he said with a careless gesture of his hand that nevertheless gave him dignity. "Your mother is suffering, and your father, excuse me, such a man I don't understand." I nodded, not wanting to get him started on my father. He coughed, turned to go, then stopped.

"What is it?" I knew he wanted to ask me something.

"Tell me . . ." He sat down heavily on the chair near the bed. He took a deep breath. "You said you saw the angel. You truly saw it?"

"Yes. I think so."

"You think so." His voice bristled.

"I did. I really did, Grandpa."

"It spoke to you?"

"No."

That seemed to satisfy him. "You imagined it."

"I don't think so."

He squirmed in his chair. "But if God would send an angel to this poor house, if He truly did, why should He give you alone the power to see it? I am closer to Him, I pray to Him every day in the year, already for over sixty years. Why should it appear to you only?"

"I don't know, Grandpa." I sighed, watching his perplexed face, the exhaustion in his eyes. I thought of his believing, year after year, when everywhere around him the world was changing. Soon he would die, my grandmother too, and what would happen? Would their ideas and beliefs die? In the streets nearby, older people, Italians mostly, sometimes spoke in another language. They would sing, too. I would often play in those streets, and the air sounded with shouts I couldn't understand. Fat ladies and skinny men and skinny and fat the other way around hobbled in and out of dark hallways jabbering away in a high rapid music. Then, on my own street, I would hear another kind of jabber mixed with words I could understand, as though one language was struggling with the other. It all sounded funny. I guess they be-

33

lieved in all the things they brought over with them—the candles and baking and holidays and awful funerals. But mostly joy. Even in the dark houses, facing the alleyways, even in the streets where their children's children played, growing into the ways of another land, they still clung to their own ways. What would happen when all the old people from the old countries died here? There would be a different life in the houses, I knew that. Different forever.

I knew I would miss my grandfather, and right now I didn't want to hurt him. He looked at me with deep hollow eyes. I wanted to comfort him, my heart flowed toward him. "Maybe I didn't see an angel after all," I said. "It happened so quick, and the white curtain moved, maybe it was the curtain . . ." I didn't want to believe it. I didn't want it to be true. It couldn't be true anyway. An angel was not a real thing. It was in the Bible and fairy tales, and sometimes in songs where girls were like angels, but what did that prove? No, I imagined it, because they were singing about angels, and the wineglass was there, waiting . . .

"All right," he said, rising. "We won't talk about it anymore. And don't please talk about it in the street. An angel is sacred. God does not like little boys talking about angels like they were potatoes, you understand?"

"Yes, Grandpa."

"So . . . good night." He reached into his pocket and withdrew a coin. "Here's ten cents for a Happy Holiday."

"Gee, thanks, Grandpa." I reached up to kiss his cheek.

"No more angels!" His voice was now imperious, but not unkind. He walked out with little shuffling steps.

I finished reading a Frank Merriwell book in less than an hour, undressed, and got into bed. I tried not to think of the angel, but all of a sudden it popped into my mind:

34

the halo! He didn't have one! If it was Elijah, a messenger of God, shouldn't he have worn a halo? I didn't remember a halo. Then it was . . . the curtains moving. I tried hard to go to sleep so I would stop thinking, but the harder I tried the more wide-awake I remained.

I didn't hear my mother enter. The room was dark and she sat at the edge of the bed, her body shook with brief silent spasms of weeping. Should I pretend to be asleep? Her hand touched my forehead.

I spoke. "I'm all right, Momma. Don't worry."

"Terrible, terrible," she murmured. "He's so hard to live with. I married him, I must have loved him. But what he did tonight I will never forgive. Never. To shame my own father, to make fun of what other people believe . . ." She squeezed my hand, and continued, "And not to believe you, his own son, is the worst thing of all."

"Did you believe me?" There was a hush in the room. "Yes."

My heart tripped with joy. "You believe I saw the angel?"

"Of course."

"But why didn't anyone else see it? Why didn't Grandpa see it, the way he talks to God practically every day?"

My mother's voice was soothing in the darkness. "Because nobody else wanted to believe it like you did. You wanted to see the angel so much that he came to you. There are angels everywhere, good and bad, beautiful and ugly, and you can call them. Not everyone can. But you can. And tonight, you saw what nobody else in the world saw."

I was dazzled by this thought. It made me sleepy. My mother said, "I will always believe what you say." She kissed me and left the room. I never remembered such happiness.

I fell asleep, and awoke with a start. Was it a minute

or hours later? A thought, running inside my head, seemed to stop before my eyes, asking me to do something. I slipped into my pants, walked down the hallway and into the living room. The house was asleep and dark. I could hear the big clock ticking like a heartbeat. I turned on the lamp. The big table was in disarray. Plates, coffee cups, and pieces of matzah lay scattered on the tablecloth. And one glass of wine. His wine!

I walked slowly to the glass, I moved close to it, my face very close, my eyes narrowing to the level of the liquid inside. How still everything was! I stared at the level: the wine seemed slightly lower in the glass. A faint ring, just above the liquid, went round the glass. That space between the ring and the liquid was Elijah's drink. Or had someone shaken the table, leaving the mark? No, it was Elijah. The proof in the glass. Believing is seeing!

Next thing—*bang!*—I woke to a blazing light on the window. I had no recollection of getting back to my room. I dressed and hurried downstairs. The table had been cleared, the wineglass gone. Was it a dream, my coming down during the night? I couldn't remember, it was all becoming unreal in the sharp morning light. Without taking my breakfast I ran into the street. At that moment, Jimmy trotted by, his arms jackknifed against his chest like a long-distance runner, tongue lolling from his mouth.

I shouted to him, and he stopped. "Guess what, Jimmy? I had a dream. You'll never guess. It was an angel. Yeah, visiting our house. I swear."

"A lady angel?" he leered. "With clothes or naked?"

"It was Elijah," I said, my voice now low.

"Too bad!" He brayed like a jackass. "Maybe next time he'll bring his sister." We laughed and raced off to the beach together, the sun spreading into our bones, hoping for some excitement during the day.

5

"To press a suit is easy after fifty years," said Mr. Perl, the tailor, slapping the garment as he stamped on the foot treadle, his body lifted for a moment off the floor. "After fifty years everything is easy, even blowing your nose. You agree, boy? But to deliver a suit isn't so easy. To carry a suit clean and pressed is a trick, so it don't drag on the floor. Listen to what I say. Are you listening?"

Working in the lockers wasn't my only job during the summer; I also helped out Mr. Perl when he was busy.

I inhaled the dry heat of the store and watched his feet moving like an organist over the steam valves, the clothes on the machine puffing with air, caught in the jaws of the presser to come out flat and smoking. His face was slightly yellowed, his eyes dim; only the quickness of his arms and legs brought him to life for me. He'd toss his head as he worked, and toss his wisdom toward the door where I waited, yearning to be elsewhere.

The trolley tracks that ran past his store began humming. The hum rose, sang, shivered, and raced through my body while the trolley came closer, weaving on the spindly rails. It seemed to be coming straight through the walls. Then it swept by, its bell hammering, suspended, quivering into silence.

"Are you listening, boy?" he called out.

"Yes. Yes, I am, Mr. Perl," I said.

"You'll find to be out in the world is no joke," he went on. "It's no Mardi Gras, but sticks and stones. You don't sneak in anywhere without a ticket. Money, my friend, money." He winked with a watery eye as he reached up to the overhead racks strung along the ceiling. How I'd marvel at his agility to reach up with the pole and deftly bring down the correct suit! He'd never be wrong, never miss. "Now, deliver this suit to Mr. Rizzo, the address is on the ticket. An Italian. Watch out he don't stick you maybe with a knife." He winked again.

I left the store carefully carrying the garment. Did Mr. Rizzo have a knife? Did all Italians carry knives? I knew one Italian boy in school, he wore a tiny cross around his neck. When we played basketball, a thin chain would slip out from under his shirt and a little gold cross would shine at the end of it. I used to watch the cross bounce at the end of the chain and wonder if it brought him luck. Whenever he made a good shot, I figured the cross helped him. Jimmy Berkowitz said the cross kept off the evil eye, but only for the Gentiles. If you were Jewish it didn't do anything.

38

I wondered if Mr. Rizzo wore a cross, because the knife idea scared me a little. I rang the Rizzo bell at a rundown frame house. A short fat man opened the door. "I'm delivering a suit," I stammered.

"You think I'm blind?" he said gruffly. He took the suit from my grasp, plunged his hand into his pocket and brought out a fistful of coins—and there was a knife! I turned and ran. "Hey kid, here's a tip," I heard him shout, but I was in the hallway and boom out of the door and into the street. I ran back to the tailor shop, out of breath. "He had a knife. I saw it!"

Mr. Perl nodded, then burst into laughter. "Mr. Rizzo wouldn't touch a fly, even a dead fly. So why are you worried?"

"But you told me—"

"Don't believe people. The first thing, when you hear something, right away shake your head. It could be a lie. Even from me. Even your father or mother."

"No, not my mother."

He stabbed a finger at me. "I know your mother. She don't know if it's raining or sunshine or if yesterday was Tuesday, a *mishugana.* Don't believe her either."

"Then who do I believe?" I asked, my eyes wavering.

He took his foot off the steam treadle and leaned on the shiny hand bar of the press. "In everybody is a voice. You know what is a voice? Not a *geshrai,* but quiet, a quiet voice only you can hear it."

"Who is it, the voice?"

He stamped on the treadle impatiently. "Who is it? You! It's you, dummkopf. In your own head. It speaks only to you. It tells you what to believe. So when somebody like a policeman smiles at you, the voice says he's a *momser,* a Cossack, let him drop dead where he stands!" Mr. Perl listened to his words echoing in the small crowded shop and nodded emphatically.

I didn't know what he was talking about, or who a Cossack was, but I liked to listen. And he would listen to me, I could ask him questions that bothered me. When I asked my father a question, he thought about it for too long, while my mother didn't think at all, she just let any old answer pop out of her head. But Mr. Perl thought just enough, you'd count up to five and he'd have an answer.

There was one question I wanted to ask him very much. It was about lying, why so many people lied everywhere, straight lies, crooked lies, smiling lies, it seemed everybody everywhere had this habit. One day I watched him sew a button on a coat, his needle flashing in a crisscross that never once missed.

"Why do people lie so much?" I asked.

He paused. "It must be. You lie to live."

"And if you always told the truth?"

He bit off the thread. "You'd die—just like that! The air would go out of your lungs!" He handed me the coat. "This is a hurry job, don't stop to pick your nose." He turned his gaze upon me. "Did you collect the money for the suit yesterday?"

"You mean Mr. Rizzo?"

"Moses I don't mean."

"Gee, I forgot. I guess when I saw the knife in his hand—"

He clucked like a hen. "Was it open or closed, the knife?"

"It was closed."

"So you're a dummy. A little closed knife, and you run. Please run back and collect from him thirty cents." And the steam billowed up around him as he stepped on the treadle.

The next day, after a delivery, I returned to find the pressing machine turned off and Mr. Perl in the back of

40

the store. He was lying on a small couch facing the wall, with rolls of cloth pushed to one side. Curled up, he looked like a funny kind of dwarf. I thought he was asleep and started to tiptoe out of the room.

"Who's there?" his voice asked softly, and he turned.

"It's me. I delivered the jacket. Mr. Hendler says he'll pay tomorrow."

He looked at me. His bald head was shining, and his eyes too. "And if he don't pay me tomorrow? Will it matter? It's too late. You know what it means, too late?" He closed his eyes and turned his face away. "Except the truth is never too late. How can a man live so long like me when he knows, he knows . . . Do you think I would be in this store another day if I told the truth? I would be dead." His voice broke in anguish. I thought for a moment he was going to cry.

I asked, "Can I get you some water?"

"Why do I need water?"

"You look pale, honest, Mr. Perl."

He rose slowly to his feet, a hand gripping the edge of the couch. "I'm pale, yes. I'm pale in my heart, in my lungs, my liver, everywhere. Because my whole life is a lie. My wife, may she rest in peace, wanted me to leave here long ago. Where to go? I didn't know where to go."

Just then the bell rang in the store and Mr. Perl went forward to see who had entered. It was Mr. Alberg, he had left his cane the day before. Mr. Alberg, older than Mr. Perl, had a cane with a ferocious bulldog head. He liked to scare kids with that head, he'd hold it near you and bark. He barked at me lots of times on the street but I pretended I didn't hear him. Once I barked back and Mr. Alberg got mad and swung the cane but I ducked and ran off. He picked up his cane and glared at me as I walked in from the back of the store.

"Some chess later?" he called to Mr. Perl.

"Go home, Alberg. I don't feel good."

"Tonight then, after work?"

"Tonight, maybe. After I close the shop. Come back."

"I owe you seventy cents." He shuffled to the door, stroking the dog head on the cane, and uttered a little bark as he left. I started to leave after him, but Mr. Perl stopped me.

"Where are you going, boy?"

"Home."

"First go and bring me a bottle of gasoline."

"Gasoline for what, Mr. Perl?" I asked.

"For stains. What else? To drink, you thought? Here's money." And his eyes brightened for a brief instant.

I brought the gasoline in a milk bottle, then walked home, thinking all the time of his talk about truth and lies. They say George Washington always told the truth, and it didn't kill him. He lived to be very old with his hair all white. But Lincoln, didn't he tell the truth about slavery, and wasn't he shot?

I brought up the subject at dinner time. My mother told me Mr. Perl was a little crazy, everyone knew it.

"He says maybe you are a little also," I ventured.

"That's how you can tell a crazy person," replied my mother evenly. "He thinks everybody else is crazy." She suddenly waved to someone through the window and dashed out. She was always waving out of the window, or else someone was waving in. It was impossible to have a long conversation with my mother, she just wasn't in one spot long enough.

My father remarked cautiously that Mr. Perl was all right but poisoned by years of inhaling cleaning fumes. As for lying, he said everybody lied a little, it was like breathing. If you breathed in too many lies, it could kill you.

"But Mr. Perl says the truth kills you," I exclaimed.

42

My father thought about it, said nothing, picked up a hammer and saw and went back to installing a new closet for a tenant. I was alone. Outside the window facing the alleyway, I could hear my mother's laughter and other voices shrilly interjecting. It was an argument of some sort, maybe about a rent payment, and her laughter meant that she was going to win the argument. She was pretending it was a joke, that's how she won most of her arguments. I shut the window and pulled down the shade. I remembered what Mr. Perl said about the voice inside you that tells you what to believe. I sat on a chair and listened for the voice. I listened so hard I could hear my heart beating, but no voice. Aah, maybe he was really nuts, except if he was he couldn't keep track of all the suits and coats in the store. And there was no point in thinking about George Washington and Abraham Lincoln, that was history. Besides, Mr. Perl was only a tailor, why try to figure out what he meant? Pretty soon I got a headache from all this and decided to go to bed.

My bedroom was in the newer part of the house, upstairs in a small corner room. I undressed and slipped under the thin sheet. It was a warm night with high humidity, and a film of dampness clung to the walls. Faintly, I could hear my father's saw whining through wood. It seemed to come from the floor below. Or was it just down the hall, three rooms away? Come out, come out, wherever you are! I used to think if someone got lost in the house during one of the many alterations, he could easily be boarded up and never found again. Now my father was enlarging a closet, working in the darkness with a droplight and extended electrical cord, and I could see him deep inside the skeletal interior, trying to steal a part of some other tenant's closet or kitchen or bathroom on the other side of the wall. And then I saw him breaking through a secret panel into a strange labyrinth of beam and girder, wire and pipe, into a small chamber that no one knew existed, not even the Building Department. He seemed far away, as though in space. A dreadful premonition touched me. I wanted to call out, but I realized he would not hear me. And as he stepped forward into the depths of the chamber, an opening yawned, down he plunged, the cord trailing after him, down into the spaces between walls and floors falling endlessly away into a jungle of steel cable and crisscrossing pipes like vines . . . I heard his scream.

I opened my eyes. It was very dark and still in the room. My forehead was damp. I felt a piercing flood of joy that the dream was over, but the scream flowed into a steady siren tone. I leaped out of bed and rushed to the window. Then I heard the fire truck and saw, at the end of the street, a dark red flame licking the air. I opened my door. Someone hissed *Fire!* and hurried down the stairway.

I put on my clothes quickly and went into the street. There was a red moon in the sky, I thought for a minute the moon had caught fire. Windows had opened, lights were on and heads were sitting on all the windowsills like pumpkins. I started walking to the end of the street as another fire truck screamed around the corner, its bell clanging right through my ears until they hurt. Up ahead I heard the crash of glass.

It was then I saw the crowd. And the store breathing out smoke in great spurts! Above the door transom the flame was being sucked upward by the air. I had to hurry and tell Mr. Perl his store was burning. Then I saw him, at the edge of the crowd, transfixed, a shawl around his shoulders. The light from the flame danced in his eyes. He looked straight into the flame, his head bobbing slightly like the head on a doll connected by a coiled spring. I ran to him and shook his arm.

44

He looked at me. "So . . . what do you want?"

"The fire!" I shook him again.

"The fire. You never saw a fire before?" His mouth twitched, and a thin trickle of saliva hung at his lips.

"All the suits are inside. All the coats and pants—"

He chimed in wildly. "And overcoats and fancy sports jackets! And hats. Hats in boxes! And the stains! Ha, ha, the stains will be burned away. Stains everywhere, do you hear me, boy?" The water was now pouring out of the fire hoses and through the broken glass into the store.

"Maybe I ought to rush in and save some things. Do you want me to, Mr. Perl?" My teeth were chattering.

"There's nothing in there. Nothing." He let out a cry. "The cane! Alberg's cane, with the dog head, he left it last night!" Now I knew he was nuts. Imagine, worrying about that lousy cane with the whole place burning! He rattled on, "It's from the old country, poor Alberg. Go in, near the sink, in the corner." I spun around, I liked the old man enough to try. Then he shouted, "No, no, you'll be killed!" He took three or four steps toward the store, stumbled, and gasped for breath. He was right alongside, his arm fell across my shoulder, then something terrible happened because he kept falling, heavily, dragging me with him to the ground. I heard a rattle in his throat and shouted, "Help, help!" The crowd moved back and a cop reached down.

The next day, I visited Mr. Perl in the hospital. He was in a special room and was lying very still with his eyes open. His skin was white, papery. His lips, thin and blue, opened slightly as I came to the bedside.

"Ah, it's you. . . . They let you in?"

"I said I was your relative. I hope you don't mind."

A wan smile brushed his face. "It's all burned down, eh, you saw the place?"

"There's nothing left, Mr. Perl."

45

His fingers reached out from under the sheets and touched my arm. "It was a good fire. You liked it?"

"I was scared."

"You wanted to run in and save the suits. You didn't understand, eh?" His eyes glittered faintly.

"Understand what?"

"Listen, I'll tell you a secret." He drew himself up on one elbow. "The fire was the truth, you see? I went to work every day, every day a lie. I had to end the lie. Only I didn't know in the excitement, my heart, because I was happy last night, you see . . . ?"

Then he stopped talking, and fell back on the bed, as though he were asleep. I went out to tell the nurse he was asleep, but I knew he was dead. The truth killed him after all.

～ 6 ～

There were fights going on in the house all the time, between the tenants, between my mother and the tenants, between my father and grandfather, between my sister and me—but the strangest fights occurred between my father and mother.

Abrupt and violent, yet one could feel them coming days ahead. They were always the same. Nothing was settled. Each fight (my mother later called them friendly arguments) went over the same facts. Then it became quiet again, for weeks, months, until I could see the fight coming on again.

It always happened when someone else in the family was present, as if my parents wanted witnesses, maybe so they could talk about it afterward with someone. When my grandfather was present (he seemed to be the favorite witness), he usually got into the fight which made it worse. Grandmother, if she was there, would join the shouting and scream, "He's an animal, a dog. I warned you not to marry him!"

One evening at dinner my father mentioned a letter he had just received from an old friend who had settled in California. He mentioned the warm California climate. I knew my father hated the local weather, and I could see the fight coming. Or he would speak of money, just a few words, and I could see it coming closer. So could my mother. At such times, she pretended not to hear him and just stared ahead, waiting. It was very spooky, like they both agreed it was coming and there was nothing either of them could do about it. Maybe they didn't want to.

"What's that smell in the rear upstairs hallway?" my father asked, entering the kitchen. I was at work painting the cabinet while my mother was rearranging the dishes.

"What smell?" My mother carefully set the dishes down.

He snorted. "That's for you to know, you run the house. There is a smell upstairs. It's sickening."

"What kind of smell?" She spoke looking right at him, now challenging him. "I don't smell anything."

"When you live in garbage too long, you don't smell it," he replied calmly and went out, and I could feel the fight coming if not today, then tomorrow, or end of the week for sure.

My mother laughed weakly. "What is he talking about? Of course, he doesn't like the house, or the tenants. But there's a mortgage to pay. This house is a natural money-maker." She stacked the dishes in silence for a moment. "Run upstairs and see if you smell anything, or if your father is losing his mind."

I put down the brush and went upstairs in the rear house. I walked along the hallways, sniffing. There were cooking smells, paint smells, smells that seemed to come out of the walls, smells of dirt and soap and old rugs and old beds and just people. It seemed to be regular smells, nothing special.

I reported this to my mother. She shook her head grimly. "Your father has a wonderful imagination, only he imagines the wrong things. Thank God you're not like him."

"I feel sometimes I am, a little, Momma," I said shyly.

"Well, if you are, you'll grow out of it. One like him in the world is enough." She went back to her chores, while I continued to paint. I thought, Was I really like my father? I didn't understand him. He seemed full of secrets. Often a distant look would cross his face, he was far away in his mind, maybe California with his friend, or the South Seas. Often he would look at me and not speak. Was he ashamed of something? Maybe he was ashamed of being where he was, in a house with all the smells, with all the people he didn't like, doing the work he didn't like. Maybe all this was on his mind for years and years. Maybe that's where the fights would come from.

"And where do you think he is now?" she exclaimed. "Off for the day again!"

"Where does Poppa go when he goes off for the day?"

"Where does a man go who has nowhere to go?" She nodded triumphantly, as if to imply the emptiness of his life compared to the fulfillment of hers.

"But he always comes back by dark," I said.

"Of course," she replied. "A man who has nowhere to go always comes home. I wouldn't call your father an explorer, he's not a Columbus exactly. If he saw America, he'd sail right by." Now she laughed at the thought—or was she laughing at *him*? I couldn't really figure out how she felt about him, maybe she didn't know herself. "Now if your father wanted to win, he could. But he hasn't got the spirit." She began clearing the dishes.

"Didn't Poppa make a nice kitchen for Mrs. Tanzer?" I wanted to remind her about these things.

She sniffed. "He's good at kitchens, and closets. I'm not talking about that. I'm talking about the spirit—what you have."

"I have it?" I asked in surprise.

"You inherited it from me," she replied gayly, seizing my hands and drawing me toward her with a girlish laugh. "You're not afraid of the world. Never be afraid!"

I let her kiss me, then grabbed a piece of cake and ran out to the sidewalk, wondering what she meant. I knew I was afraid of many things, of girls, of the dark, of leaning over the roof, and the idea of never being afraid sounded silly. And there were things I thought I was afraid of without being sure. Being afraid was sometimes delicious, it made you feel someone would protect you—sometimes the same person who made you afraid! I once dreamed of a bear that came toward me with huge open arms while I waited terrified, but he didn't crush me, he hugged me and started to dance. What a dream that was! Nobody believed it.

The street had begun to bake with shimmering waves of heat. A block away, the clamor of church bells sent a flutter of pigeons into the sky. I had some chores to do—sweep the alley and the lockers, change a light bulb in the shower room—but my mind drifted away from the house.

Where was my father? Where did he go on these days? I decided to look for him. Something my mother had said . . . I wanted to find him. And so I trotted toward the boardwalk. It was the first place to go when you looked for someone, especially when that person went

50

for a walk. My father liked to walk. It was a good place to begin.

I went past Ravenhall Baths, drumming my fingers along the corrugated metal that protected the rows of lockers. I came to a peephole that Jimmy had discovered —a bolt loosened and pushed through—but a new bolt had been inserted. Jimmy and I had seen lots of fat naked ladies through that hole, and skinny ones too, but never anyone just right. We had many laughs and were chased away often. Jimmy would be sad about the missing peephole, or did he know already?

Up the street ramp and onto the boardwalk: a million people! It felt like a million. The whistle of the peanut roaster stayed above the dense rattle of shoes on the boards. I walked past stores and booths of wild colors, with fake soda bottles and wax ice-cream, then real franks, clams, oysters, with funny old men and ladies calling out their wares. Pinwheels fluttered at my ear and kewpie dolls winked in the sunshine. I walked past entrances to bath houses and outdoor pools, and along stretches of roller coaster that skirted the iron railings and roared away into dark tunnels.

My eye roved the benches for a sign of him. The beach was rapidly filling up—he would never be on the beach, he didn't like crowds, but on weekends the whole place was one big crowd.

I saw a figure sitting far out on the stone jetty, and raced across the sand to investigate. The tide was at medium height, a slime of seaspray and weed clung to the rocks and made the footing tricky. Seagulls whined and clattered above me. I had to go two-thirds of the way out before I realized it wasn't him. I retraced my steps nimbly, goat-like, and hopped back onto the hard sand.

Not far from the jetty, on high piles, a wooden pier jutted at right angle to the boardwalk out into the ocean for well over a quarter of a mile. It was the terminal of a steamboat line that made several runs a day from lower Manhattan. Fishermen lined the railing of the pier, day and night. My father wasn't interested in fishing, but he might want to get away from the beach crowd. I crossed the sand again, skipped up the steps to the boardwalk, and walked toward the pier. A boat had just docked, and its passengers moved past me as I hurried toward the docking area at the pier's end. The whistle tooted. What if my father decided to get on the boat and go away? A throb of fear rippled through me. Would he do that without saying goodbye, or leaving a note?

"Hey, you dumb kid, watch out!" A body rammed me to one side. I kept my balance and continued to the dock as the boat slowly edged away. I scanned the faces on the boat. It was foolish, because my father never liked boats.

I decided to go to the playground where men sat and played checkers and chess. I started back along the pier and then I saw him. He was seated on the bench that ran along the pier-railing. In one hand was a sheet of paper, in the other a pencil. He was writing, slowly, laboriously, holding the paper to his knee. I approached and walked by him, then turned and walked by again. His eyes were on the paper. I sat down a short distance away, half-hiding behind a fat lady with an umbrella. I didn't know if I should let him see me; he might become angry. I could go up to him and say, Poppa I wondered where you were and came to find you . . . What would he do? I shivered in anticipation and doubt. No, I'd better go back home. The lockers were waiting to be swept.

Then his head turned and he saw me. I tried to duck behind the fat lady but his eyes were still upon me (I could feel them right through her!). Sheepishly, I got up and walked toward him, my face frozen in a weak smile. He kept looking at me, expressionless, but I thought not unkindly. He fingered the paper and pencil with an uncertain motion, as though he wished to hide them.

"Hello, Poppa," I said, my throat tightening.

He nodded. "What are you doing here?"

"I just took a walk. For exercise. I like the pier."

A silence. Then, "Did your mother send you to look for me?"

I shook my head firmly. "No, Poppa, I just came by myself." He believed me. And it was the truth! Maybe my mother put the idea in my head (did she?) but I was sure I came here because I wanted to.

My father fumbled with the paper on his knee. He seemed a little embarrassed, and that made me feel easier. He looked up and asked, "Are you good at figures?"

"You mean arithmetic? Yes," I answered eagerly.

He handed me the paper and pencil. "Write down what I say." I waited, smoothing the paper against the wooden bench. Then he spoke. "Two floors in the front house, five rooms on each floor. That makes ten rooms. Rear house, ten more, not counting kitchens and the lockers. Average two rooms for us through the year. That leaves eighteen rooms for income, say four dollars average per week each room . . . how much is that? Per week?"

I quickly multiplied the figures. "Seventy-two."

"A month would be . . ."

"Counting four weeks to a month, it would be two hundred and eighty-eight. If you count strictly by the week—"

"Let's say two hundred fifty each month."

My fingers sped over the page, anticipating the next question. "Three thousand dollars a year."

"And seven years?"

"Twenty-one thousand."

He repeated the figure slowly. "Twenty-one thousand
. . . Where is it? Even counting the mortgage payments
and our food, where is that money? What happened to
twenty-one thousand dollars? We have no money. Where
is it?" I shook my head, although he wasn't speaking to
me. He rose, his voice hoarse. "Who did she give it to?
A friend? Her brothers? Her father?"

I didn't know what to say. "Can we get a root beer,
Poppa?" I stammered.

"Get some for yourself. Here's a nickel." He gave me
a coin, then stood looking out across the water for a
whole minute without moving. "I'm going back, Poppa,"
I said. He nodded vaguely, and kept looking out at the
water where, far off, a white sail danced in the sunlight.

I didn't buy the root beer, hurrying home instead to
sweep the lockers. As I worked, I could hear through the
wall of the living room the voices of my mother and
grandfather. When I came in, they lowered their voices
and moved to the other end of the room, speaking softly.
I sensed something was going to happen. My father
entered, went to the bureau, opened it, and pretended to
look inside. Something unheard suddenly gathered in the
air. Then I knew it was going to happen. The fight.

Turning to Grandfather in a conversational way, my
father asked, "Did you come for the money today?"
There was a silence. Grandfather stiffened and slowly rose
to his feet. It was happening now. My father continued,
"I'm asking you a question. Did you come for the
money?" And he spoke the last words slowly.

My mother darted a look in my direction, but I pretended not to be listening.

"I don't know anything about money," replied Grandfather.

"You know about it, especially about counting it.
Counting it and hiding it. Where do you hide it, old

man?" Now his voice became cold and level and cruel.

My mother cut in. "Leave him alone, please."

He spun around. "You want to answer for him? Then answer. Did he take any money today?"

"What do you want?" she wailed.

"Where is the money you've been giving him all these years? I want an answer!" He pounded the table.

This was the fight, the same fight, the same subject, and it would have the same ending.

My father kept on. "Where is the money? Are you hiding it? Are you losing it, you fool? You mad woman. For years this house has been bringing in a profit. Where is it? We are living in a pigsty, with whores, we have no home, no meals on time, no family, but we have the money to get out and live somewhere else. Where is it? Has he got it all, this old faker with his prayers?" He turned to Grandfather, his eyes blazing.

"Don't you dare insult him!" my mother screamed.

"He's a thief. A religious thief, they're the worst!" my father retorted. "He has been robbing me for years. He has been forcing you to give him the money, you're frightened to death of him. He should be in jail!"

Grandfather groaned and shuddered visibly. I couldn't believe he would steal. And why would my mother steal from her own husband? Maybe my father was making it up. Grandfather took a step toward the door. "God is waiting for you," he said. "For judgment."

"The devil is waiting for you!" thundered my father.

At that point (usually when God came into it) my mother uttered a cry and fell to the floor in a faint. Then my father left the room. I ran for a glass of water, bent down and placed the glass to her lips. She moaned, sipping at the water. My grandfather kept muttering, "How will it end? How will it end?" After a moment, my mother sat up, then slowly rose and walked to the couch where she lay down and closed her eyes. Soon she was asleep. Grandfather turned to me. "Watch her. She's married to a heathen." And he walked out.

I was alone. My mother slept. She would sleep for an hour sometimes after the fight. Then she woke. "I'll be all right," she whispered hoarsely. Soon after, she picked up her work again. Her voice remained at a whisper for days. Then, gradually, it would grow stronger, and within a week she would be calling out to neighbors and tenants while my father went about his work calmly, both acting as though nothing had happened. Grandfather would drop in again for a cup of tea, chatting amiably, pretending all was well. Until the next time.

It was a fight that never ended, that never explained anything, and made everyone feel better for a while. I used to think it was a kind of a game, even my mother's fainting, because she did it so neatly and got better so soon. Still, for several days afterward, she turned away when our eyes met.

There were mornings when I woke to the sound of the hammer and saw, and mornings when I woke to silence. I could still tell, on the silent days, when my father was working somewhere in the house: he left a trail of wood shavings, the odor of a cigar, or neat piles of cut boards in the alley or hallway.

My father would be busy with alterations for weeks at a time. It wasn't that the house was falling apart, but there was the problem of fitting it to different tenants. If a small family moved in needing two or three rooms, my father would break through the walls or partitions of single rooms to make an apartment. Then it might happen that a single room was needed, and a partition would go up again. There were other problems, such as

57

being short a kitchen, or once in a while somebody had a room with an extra bath left over from an earlier apartment, or elsewhere an extra kitchen remained boarded up, kept out of sight until needed. And closets, I don't know how we kept track of them; a closet converted into a small kitchen, then presto—back into a closet again! It was easy with small gas stoves and flexible hosing that snaked around a wall to feed into a main line. Easy, I mean, if you kept track of where things were before you changed them.

I remember my father removing a partition that was supposed to open into dead space but actually opened into occupied living quarters. Suppose it had opened into a bathroom, maybe while someone was taking a bath? You never knew what would happen once you broke into a wall.

The Building Department was supposed to know about each new alteration. You had to file a plan first, and then it would be approved, and later an inspector would arrive and check the new construction to make certain it met the requirements of the Building Code. In the early years, with large new additions, my father would follow these rules. But with later and smaller construction— closet, kitchen, moving a wall or two—he neglected to notify the department. Things had to be done on the spot, with no time to wait for approval. Once, a stairway was moved several feet to allow a small bathroom to be fitted snugly in the space beneath. This was not reported until an inspector stumbled on it a year later during a routine checkup on another job. He came back soon after with a sheaf of blueprints, looking very mad, and my father had to put up some special beam supports to make sure the bathroom was safe for traffic.

My mother joked about the incident, but the inspector came back often after that stairs business. I bet our blueprints drove the Building Department crazy, they were always trying to make the blueprints match the house.

I enjoyed helping my father with these chores. I learned a lot about plumbing and electricity and how to fix water faucets and burnt-out fuses. I liked the fuse emergency the best. I knew just where the replacement fuses were hidden, and whenever the house darkened, I hurried to the basement with a flashlight, found the bad fuse, and replaced it with the new one, my eye on the voltage wheel that would suddenly start to turn again. From far below, like magic, I sent up light with a twist of my fingers!

In midsummer, a special alteration job was decided upon. I followed my father to the lumberyard. He examined the boards carefully, his eye alert for warping and dangerous wood knots. He knew everything about lumber, especially how to cut it and match it, and how to use the saw correctly. Often he would begin the cut on a board and let me continue it through. I loved the sound of the steel teeth grunting against the wood, the low guttural changing to a whine as the saw moved across the board toward the edge. Cutting the edge clean was the hardest part; you had to ease up on the blade thrust and give only the weight of the blade to the final inch. If you pressed too much, the final bit of wood might snap off, thus impairing the board and spoiling a perfect join. I was also very careful to follow the pencil guide-mark; at times the blade would strike stubbornly across the grain, and I had to fight it for a straight cut. My father would hold a T square against the cut edges. If I was off the mark a bit, he'd correct it with the saw or a heavy-rasped wood file; if I made a perfect cut, he accepted it without a word, but I knew he was pleased.

He never spoke much. When someone is quiet, you have to guess at what he's thinking. Everybody guessed about my father, especially relatives and neighbors; nobody knew for sure. While my mother talked all the time and left you confused, my father said little, sometimes only a few sentences for the whole day. Maybe, I thought, he was secretly angry at someone (was it me?). Or could it be he didn't like to talk, like the Indian chief in a movie I saw who smiled and only said "Ugh"? Except my father hardly ever smiled. Still, he could have been an Indian, I bet, and look out over the prairie without saying a word, or maybe saying something like, "You come for peace, we share land." Would my Indian-father scalp anyone? He carried a sharp-edged hatchet in his toolbox, even without being an Indian, and I thought if he were an Indian he'd have a fancy hatchet all right. Yes, but would he use it? It was scary just to think of it!

For this particular alteration, my father didn't wait for delivery but carried the lumber on his shoulder all the way home from the lumberyard without getting tired. I trotted alongside, listening to the slap-slap of the thin boards as they bounced softly to his walking rhythm. They were twelve-foot boards. If I were carrying them, they would have struck people or branches whenever I turned a corner, but my father knew just how to turn, easily, almost carelessly, without touching anything.

We arrived at the house. I skipped up the back stairs to the first landing, leaned out on the fire escape, and received the boards handed up to me from the street level. Then I hoisted each board in a sweeping motion to rest against the window of the landing above. My muscles ached. This was the exciting part. I was really needed here, he couldn't do it without me.

After the boards were hauled in through the top-floor window, my father marked them according to a layout plan and cut them to size. I held the long boards steady to prevent them from binding the saw. I knew just how to do that. Ready for nailing, he reached down into his tray of nails. Then he turned and said, "Run down to the hardware and bring two pounds of eight-penny nails. I'm getting low." Before he had finished speaking I was in motion. I bounded down the stairs, into the street, my sneakers gripping the pavement as I sprinted to the hardware store.

I spotted a few friends on the way, but didn't stop to talk. Mr. Litzik waved to me from inside the bakery shop, but I breezed by. I had no time to make any deliveries for Mr. Litzik when I was on an important errand. I passed Mr. Alberg who shook his cane at me as usual. I leapfrogged two fire hydrants in a row, swung around a telephone pole, did a leaping broad jump, dodged a Chevrolet truck, and arrived at the store run by Mr. Farber. I barked out my order.

"What are the nails?" asked Mr. Farber. He had very thick glasses and his eyes bulged like fish eyes looking at you from a tank.

"Just nails," I said.

"Carpet tacks is also nails," he said, blinking from behind the glasses. "You have a size?"

"Gee, I forgot the size."

Mr. Farber nodded as though my reply was to be expected. "In college you'll also forget." I was embarrassed and looked down at the floor just in time to see a cockroach race under a barrel. I heard him say, "What is your father doing that he needs the nails?"

"Alteration with one-by-threes," I answered.

"With one-by-threes could be eight-penny or ten-penny or even sixteen-penny," he mused, watching me like he was a teacher expecting me to solve a problem in arithmetic.

The numbers confused me. I knew sixteen-penny was wrong. I wasn't sure of eight-penny. Ten seemed right. "I'll have the ten," I said.

"Take a pound each."

"No, I'll take number ten."

He tossed handfuls of nails on a balance scale, into a scarred metal bucket at one end. When the loaded bucket started to raise the other weighted end, he paused, watching the wavering balance severely through his glasses. His fingers dropped the nails one at a time until he got a perfect balance. Then gallantly, wearily, he threw in two more nails and poured them all into a bag. As I dashed out I saw him write something in a small notebook.

On my way back, Mr. Litzik waved his fist at me and beckoned with his finger. Same to you, Litz the Fritz! I laughed gleefully and sped by his store.

My father sifted the nails with his fingers and looked at me. "I said eight-penny nails, weren't you listening?" His eyes were hard.

"I thought it was ten, I thought you said ten," I whispered.

"Because you don't listen. Your mother can't listen and you're like her." He was angry, although he didn't raise his voice.

"I guess I . . . I forgot. I'll go back to the store."

"I'll go this time. You stay here. Get in the closet and watch the tools. Go on."

I backed into the opening where the tools lay scattered on the floor. I wanted to speak but my tongue froze. My father moved a sheet of plywood across the opening. He was going to board up the closet! With sinking heart I heard his hammer drive in two nails to hold the plywood in place. I cried out, "I forgot, Poppa. I didn't mean to . . ." My voice choked with fear.

"You stay in there. Next time listen to what I say." And his footsteps vanished.

I could hear my heart pounding. The dark and the silence enveloped me. I pressed against the plywood. If I pushed hard enough the nails would loosen, but I was afraid he would be even angrier. I had to wait. I stood motionless. After a moment I reached out an arm and touched something that sent a shiver through me. It was a pipe covered with a slimy film. I moved away and stumbled against the toolbox. My eyes slowly recognized the dim form of the interior, with a jagged area ripped open for enlargement. Some of the flooring had been torn up. I was afraid to move, afraid I might trip into the flooring space and fall through. I'd vanish. They would look for me and never find me.

I remembered the dream I once had of my father, and now it was I falling into the black spaces between the walls, reaching out to break my fall but finding only emptiness, and down I plunged past the basement into the earth which appeared to open into another house and I falling endlessly . . .

"Help," I moaned. "Save me, Poppa!" My voice startled me. My teeth began to chatter. I gripped a beam, my eyes shut. Closing my eyes seemed to help. I began to count, ten, twenty, to a hundred. I thought of my teacher Mrs. Reber, and all the maps of the world I drew in her class, with rivers and industries.

I grew quiet. The darkness held unseen creatures. I heard a low scurrying at my feet. Soon I heard the wiry buzz of a mosquito. I was relieved, even happy, I didn't even care if I was bitten. I started to laugh at the idea of the mosquito being locked in the dark with me, but the laugh sounded high and strange and I stopped. Where was my father? What if he forgot to come back? I heard muffled voices from the other side of the wall. Should I call out? No, no, he'd hate me if I told! I would lose everything.

I tried to control my breathing, inhaling slowly, deeply, which helped the time pass. Footsteps approached. They came to a stop at the plywood. Then the claw of a hammer gripped the nails and yanked them free. The plywood fell back.

I didn't look at him, nor did he say anything to me. I snaked past him and hurried down the stairs that led into the alleyway. Jimmy Berkowitz popped his head out of the locker room and whistled. "Psst. I got somethin' in the ladies locker, fat lady under a shower!" I ran by him and all the way to the beach, far out on the jetty, almost into the water, before I stopped.

I sat watching a ship move across the horizon until it fell out of sight. Questions exploded inside my head. Why was my father so different from my mother? Did they love one another? And if they didn't, what would happen to me? It began to grow dark. A gull settled close by and stared at me. I got tired of thinking and walked back home.

Dinner was quiet. The food had no taste in my mouth. "What's the matter with you?" asked my mother. "Are you sick?"

"Nothing's the matter," I replied in a low voice, my eyes down.

"What happened today?" She turned toward my father, who was finishing his coffee.

"Are you talking to me?" he asked her.

"I have the honor," she said tartly.

"I have nothing to say."

"Your son isn't happy."

"You're happy enough for all of us." My father rose, pushing the coffee cup to one side.

"Say something to the boy!" my mother demanded.

I lifted my eyes. His face was impassive. He started for the door. "When I ask for eight-penny nails," he said in his slow careful voice, "I want eight-penny."

And he walked out.

~ 8 ~

Of all the people who moved into our house, I guess I remember Philip the best. He was older than I, about fourteen, sad-eyed, skinny, and had to spend most of the time in a wheelchair. He had something we'd never heard of before on our block: an enlarged heart. Pretty soon we called him Jumpy because his heart could be seen jumping right under his skin when his shirt was open. The spot on his chest would go *poom-boom poom-boom* (without a sound) up and down, no bigger than a dime. It was weird. Yet after a while we got used to it. Watching it was like a game.

When Jumpy was wheeled out in his chair on the sidewalk to sit in the morning sun, he'd wave his arm and call, "It's me, fellas." And we'd crowd around, joshing him, spinning his chair, until someone would say, "Let's see it jump, how about it, Jumpy!" And grinning shyly, he opened his shirt, as we stared at the pulsing circle of flesh—his real alive heart!

Jumpy smiled feebly. "The doctor says I'll get better. I might even go back to school after summer vacation." We said nothing; we didn't know much about hearts, but it didn't look as though he would be in school for a long time.

I would stop into his room almost every day. He sat up in bed, reading or listening to the radio, or just leaning back looking into space. I would sometimes come in and he wouldn't see me, and the room so silent I'd think he was dead. I'd call out, "Jumpy?" And he would turn slowly, his eyes brightening. "Hi, sit down."

We talked about all kinds of things. Baseball and horses and radios. He had a small crystal set. We wondered how music came from an inch of wire probing a piece of crystal—with no electricity! We talked about school, science, and the tutor who came to the house. That was before he got too sick and stopped studying altogether. We played cards a lot.

His mother was nice, but sad, as if she knew something was going to happen. She brought us cakes and ice cream while we played our games. They had to be quiet games because he couldn't get excited; that made it worse, his mother explained.

Sometimes my sister would visit. She was shy, and she usually brought him some little gift, like a jelly-apple or a bag of cherries. He loved cherries.

"You look better, Philip," my sister said on these visits. (She never called him Jumpy; she used his real name.)

"Thank you," Jumpy replied.

"You look much better than last week, honest, Philip," she said. And he smiled his thin but intense smile. He never said much to her. She, as well, was embarrassed. She was skinny in her bathing suit and had small knobby breasts. She was shy all the time. I was conscious of her growing up, and it made me feel a little strange at first. I found myself watching her more after that. I saw her sleeping once, naked, but I didn't hang around—I was just getting something from the room. Anyway, her growing up and Jumpy's growing up made them shy with each other. I thought he liked her, but I wasn't sure about what she felt.

Once, when we were talking about girls, Jumpy said he thought my sister was a nice kid.

"Did you ever kiss a girl?" I asked him.

"No. Did you?"

"Yes," I said.

"I don't mean sisters," he said.

I had, in fact, earlier that summer, kissed a slender light-haired girl good night. It wasn't much of a kiss, but I recalled the warmth of her lips with a shiver. It was quick; in the movies they were long kisses, but I suppose that was for older people. Anyway, standing on the stoop was bad for your balance, and that slender girl and I just brushed faces, you might say. Still, I wasn't lying when I said I had kissed a girl.

"What was it like?" he wanted to know.

I scratched my head and gulped one of the cherries. "It was like . . . very different. I wouldn't know how to describe it, Jumpy. All I can say is, I'd do it again if I got the chance."

"I'd sure like to try it," said Jumpy. "But I guess you gotta ask a girl. They just won't come over and kiss you, would they?"

I shook my head. "I don't think so. I never heard of it. Maybe if it was something special they would."

"Well, anyway . . ." Jumpy's voice trailed off. "It

ain't going to happen to me, I guess." We continued to play cards.

Later, alone with her, I asked my sister, "What do you think about Jumpy?"

"You mean Philip? I hate that nickname. He's too nice to have such a nickname."

"Do you like him?"

"Oh, he's all right." She looked at me curiously. "Why?"

"Nothing. Only he asks about you a lot. He's goofy about you."

She simpered. "You know what you are? You're absolutely cuckoo," she said.

I shot back at her, "He'd love to smooch with you. He keeps saying he'd *love* to kiss you. What about *that*?"

"I am not interested in kissing Philip," she said imperiously. But underneath I knew the idea scared her. After all, she was just a kid, and with her little breasts she was growing up and thinking about things like kissing. I was. And so was everybody else, I figured.

I kept thinking of Jumpy, in bed most of the time, with a doctor coming by twice a week, and not once being kissed by a girl. When I thought of all the kissing going on on the beach, and under the boardwalk, and practically everywhere—well, it was a shame about Jumpy.

He took a turn for the worse. He wasn't out of the house for days. His mother wouldn't allow any of us to come into his room. Once I peeked in and saw him lying on the bed, his head turned toward the wall. I called out softly, "Hey Jumpy." He moved his head, lifted his arm weakly, but didn't turn. I went away. That night, the doctor arrived on a special visit. My mother met him in the hall and went inside the room with him. I tried to enter, but they wouldn't allow me. I listened at the door. All I could hear were muffled voices and, I thought, a sound of weeping.

The next day, when I asked my mother what happened, she only said, "He's very sick," and went about her work. I waited in the hall until Jumpy's mother came out of the room. When she saw me, she said in a whisper, "My poor little boy." She pressed my hand and went off into the street.

I pushed the door open into Jumpy's room. He was alone. I went up to the bed. I hadn't seen him for over a week, and I was shocked. His face seemed to be stretched thin like paper; the eyes had sunken deep into their sockets; the mouth was thin and blue. His pajama shirt was open, and I could see his heart leaping against his skin; in my ears it suddenly sounded *poom-boom poom-boom* louder and louder. I swallowed and the sound went away.

Jumpy saw me. "Boy, I must be sick with doctors coming around every day."

"You look OK," I lied.

"I don't know, I broke the mirror yesterday lookin'," he said, with that odd persisting smile playing around his mouth. "I must look like some kind of freaky ghost."

I didn't know what to say, because he was right. I pushed his shoulder jokingly. He sighed, leaned back on the pillow, and stared at the ceiling. "Jimmy and the guys send their regards," I said hesitatingly.

He said, "I had a dream about Jimmy. You'll never guess what it was. You won't tell him?" I shook my head. "I mean, he might think I had something against him."

"What'd you dream?" I prodded him.

"You won't laugh? I dreamed he was dead." He started to laugh, and I laughed, and we both laughed so loud I thought we'd both get a stomachache. Jumpy started to cough, and I rushed to get him some water. He choked on the water and I had to slap him on the back. Then we got to talking about some other things. Baseball. The law of gravity. And, again, girls. He asked about my sister again; she hadn't been in to say hello for over a week. I mumbled some apology for her and after a while I left.

I met my sister outside. She was sitting in the sun reading a book. I bought her an ice-cream cone. She looked up, surprised. "Where'd you get the money, Mr. Rockefeller?"

"My allowance, Miss America, ha, ha."

"You always think you're funny when you're not," she said haughtily, licking at the ice cream. We were alone on the bench, and I decided to bring up the subject again.

"I saw Jumpy just now—I mean, Philip. He asked about you." She continued reading. "I was wondering, Sis . . . would you go up and say hello? He's pretty sick."

"I might later on. I'm reading now, can't you see?"

"When you go up, would you do me a favor? Don't get mad. Would you kiss him?" She stopped her reading. Her eyes widened. "Just kiss him. Just once. Would you, please?"

"Why should I?"

"Well, he's awful sick—but it's not catching like a cold or anything. He's so blue. You'd cheer him up. Would you?"

She snapped her book shut and rose. "Please leave me alone or I'll tell Momma." And she ran into the house.

Not many days later, Jumpy's mother came over to me on the street, her eyes numb. "He's dying. Any day now, the doctor says. We mustn't feel bad. It's best with such a disease."

All that afternoon in my ear, even when I swallowed, was the sound *poom-boom poom-boom,* and any minute that heart might stop!

I spoke to my sister again, as she was leaving the kitchen after dinner. "He asked for you again."

She was skeptical. "You're making it up."

"No," I pleaded. "He's awfully lonely. If you'd see him for a minute, that's all, and just kiss him—"

"If you don't stop that—" She turned to go.

I gripped her arm. "Don't be a stuck-up. If a friend asks you for a kiss, is that a crime?"

"I don't like him."

"Do you have to *like* a fella, I mean a friend, to kiss him, just *one* kiss!"

She broke away and ran to my mother, sobbing. "I won't do it. He wants me to kiss Philip. I won't, I won't!"

My mother, startled, comforted her. "Quiet, you don't have to kiss anyone if you don't want to." She turned to me. "What is it now?"

I kept my eyes lowered. I didn't know how to explain such a thing. "I just asked her to kiss Jumpy. What's so terrible about it?" I was getting sore at my sister. "Anyway, she's a stuck-up!" I ran to the street, sullen, furious, defeated.

At bedtime, my sister came to my room. I could see she had come to be forgiven. Standing at the door, she said, "I'm sorry I told Momma on you. That was wrong." I didn't answer, I'd gotten too tired thinking of Jumpy and his heart that would stop any minute.

She didn't go. "I hope you're not mad," she said. "After all, I don't know Philip, not really, I mean . . ." Her voice trailed off in uncertainty.

"If you do it, I'll give you a dollar. I promise. Gosh, how can you say you don't know him?" She was silent.

72

"It ain't so awful kissing someone. You've kissed me lots of times."

"Kissing you is not the same, and you know it," she replied, wavering.

"It can't be much different with Jumpy. He's my age, about."

"The whole thing is silly, but I'll do it." Her acceptance, finally, was so casual I couldn't understand all the fuss she made earlier. What a screwloose for a sister, I thought! "When do I do it?" she asked.

"Right now," I said. She looked calm, as though she kissed boys every day which I don't think she did, but it crossed my mind. I didn't see her much during the day. "Come on," I said. She followed me down the hallway. We came to his door. I knocked softly. We entered. He was alone, his eyes half-closed. I thought he was asleep until he spoke.

"Hello. I'm glad you came." His eyes, now fully opened, rested on my sister. She walked to the bed, her walk light, almost jaunty. "Hi, Philip. I'm sorry I haven't been up to see you lately. But you look fine."

He smiled weakly. His face was yellowed. He opened his mouth but his voice was so low I had to lean over to hear him. "Good night," he said.

"Sure, Jumpy, we won't stay," I turned to my sister and nodded to her. "We just dropped in for a quick hello. See you again tomorrow."

"Tomorrow," he whispered. His fingers reached over but could barely grip my hand.

"See you again," said my sister. She leaned over the bed, her eyes tightly shut, her face moving close to his. With a cry, he turned his head into the pillow. My sister looked at me, her lips trembling, and fled from the room. "Get out," Jumpy shouted. "Leave me alone. I don't

73

want to see anybody!" I backed slowly toward the door, stunned by his anger.

The next afternoon, it was hard for me to imagine it was him in the coffin. I thought of his small heart quiet now under his clean shirt, and the *poom-boom* in my ear was quiet, too.

My sister cried a little. She was mad at me for a long time, for months, and wouldn't talk to me. Sometimes she'd lose her temper and scream at me even when I didn't remember doing anything wrong.

Love is a pretty big subject, and my mother seemed more mixed up about it than anybody I knew; she mixed me up, too, maybe forever. She thought everybody should love everybody else, immediately, at first sight, like in the movies.

Especially strangers—they were, to her, as God's messengers testing that divine impulse in man. Tramps and itinerants soon passed the word that our house was a soft touch. It was like the Underground Railroad I studied in school: everybody escaping to somewhere would stop by for a quick ration or, with night coming on, for a bed. There were times when I couldn't tell the regular tenants from the overnights.

If anyone needed a dollar for a nonexistent sick wife,

a dying pal, or homeless child, my mother would give the dollar. She was a shrewd and hard bargainer in other ways, but she had that thing in her head, saying, *It's love love love*. Sometimes she'd hum those words with any old tune.

It mixed me up because, first of all, to start at home, I wasn't sure she loved my father.

If a man left his wife, it was always, to her, a lover's quarrel. And when a headline told of an ax murder, MAN SLAYS BLONDE, my mother sighed and said, "He must have loved her." All this left me more confused than ever.

Even loving my mother wasn't clear to me. Often, in the middle of the day, when a sudden fear of the future would rush in upon me, when I saw myself alone in the world, she would shatter my daydream with "What's the matter, why so sad, smile and the world smiles with you," and I guessed that was part of love, her being there, effortless, always.

Lots of people on the block thought my mother was nutty. Behind her back, they often tapped their head with a finger. But my mother laughed it off. "They're jealous of me," she'd say. "I have imagination. Nothing frightens people more than imagination!" And she hugged me until her eye caught a neighbor, whereupon she thrust me aside to pick up an old argument. I believed her. She was strange, I thought, but not nutty. And imagination . . . I don't think she was sure where she was most of the time.

Her idea of imagination was leaving the door unlocked between the Men and Women shower rooms of her bathing-locker establishment. People often wandered into the wrong room, and if they weren't friendly when they arrived, some of them were when they left, I'll bet. Maybe that was love love love, too . . .

I wondered. And when those two girls, Marge and Belle, moved into a room on the middle floor, I wondered even more. They were flashy, with loud makeup, high heels, and tight clothes. My mother adored them. They left for work quite late in the morning, returned during the afternoon, and went out again at night. Often they would sit outside during the afternoon, or late at night in their tight-fitting clothes. They made a lot of friends. The talk began; neighbors would point them out, and whisper.

This gossip angered my mother. "Can't a girl have friends?" she said to a neighbor. "And can't a girl entertain friends in her room? Two girls in a room are perfectly safe."

The girls became very popular in the neighborhood, and the cluster of men around the house at night increased. Marge was the livelier one; her reddish hair caught the store lights like a halo; her feet, when she sat, kept making small circles on the pavement; she laughed easily, loudly. Belle was less forward; her face, over-rouged, seemed impassive, even hard. She listened to the men joking but rarely smiled. She took her cue from Marge; if Marge laughed, she did also. Marge would often grab one of the men around the waist and say, "Let's dance, how about it, buddy?" And they'd dance right there in front of the house, with Marge singing a tune, and the onlookers clapping hands or throwing in a gag line.

"I'd like to get Marge on a barge."

"Is it true you do it, Marge old pal?"

"Is it true you give green stamps, Marge honey?"

Marge enjoyed these remarks. She wasn't very bright. She hung her underwear on a line running high across the alley. She would lean out of the window, her mouth full of clothespins, and a neighbor would yell up to her,

"What's the time, Marge?" and she'd open her mouth to answer and the pins would sail down to the laughter below.

Both girls would tell jokes and laugh, and sometimes walk toward the beach after dark. I'd want to follow them, but my mother called me in to bed. On some nights, unable to sleep, I'd look out of my window and see Marge and Belle return each with a boyfriend. It seemed they had lots of boyfriends. I often heard a victrola in their room, and muffled laughter and singing. They were always having a party.

My mother told the neighbors they were secretaries in a big office. She took phone messages for them and insisted that it was certainly no crime to have friends. Girls like these, she once said, were sure to fall in love and get married when the right man came along.

It's love love love . . .

Each morning, when they would stumble out in the sunlight, my mother greeted them grandly. "Good morning, dears. How are you this morning? Did you sleep well? How are your beds? Do you want larger beds?" And Marge, chucking my mother under the chin, replied, "Thanks, dearie. The beds are fine. And you are, too."

One night, when the house was quite dark, a loud commotion erupted on the girls' floor. Their door banged open, and a voice yelled, "What kinda joint is this? Listen, I want my change, what the hell is this . . ." One of the girls answered, "G'wan you cheap, goddamn cheap . . . " Someone stumbled down the stairs and into the street, and it was quiet again. The noise, however, had wakened my father.

The next day, after my sister had left the kitchen, my father said, "I want you to get those whores out of the house." My mother dropped the cup she was holding. "What did you say?"

"I said get them out of the house, they're too noisy."

"What did you call them?" she demanded coldly.

"I called them what they are."

"How dare you, in front of the boy—"

My father shouted, "Don't you think he knows? Everyone knows but you. Now I want them evicted. For God's sake, you've got children growing up in the house."

"They are not what you said."

"I told you what to do!" he said sharply, and left the room. My mother called after him, "You've got a sick mind. You deserve to live alone, without friends, or a wife, or children. You should be a sailor on a ship, a ship with a leak in the middle of the ocean!" She was angrier than I ever remembered. "He never took me anywhere, not to a dance, not once. When we were married, I would dress up for a dance, I begged to go, but he laughed at me. He never had any romance, I was young and ignorant or I'd never have married him. He won't say good morning to a neighbor, he hates my tenants, and now he picks on those two lonely girls . . ."

She went on and on, but I didn't hear her. I was thinking of Marge and Belle. They were "bad" girls, that's why men always followed them, and told jokes, and smiled when they walked past. That's what it meant.

Like all these family fights, my mother never did anything after the fight—that is, she continued to do whatever she was doing. She did not evict the girls. She treated them exactly as before: they were her darlings.

One day, a mild-looking man came into the lockers while I was helping to clean up, and motioning my mother to one side, questioned her about the girls. He was, he announced, a policeman.

"Where's your uniform?" my mother asked suspiciously, half-jokingly.

"I'm a plainclothes," he said, showing his badge.

"Would you like something to drink, some lemonade?" My mother's strategy with the law always began with a beverage.

"No, thanks, lady. What I want to know is—"

"A shot of whiskey, if that's allowed, Officer, between ourselves?"

He smiled. "When I'm off duty, maybe. Right now I'm on duty."

"Who'll know?" she answered his smile.

He looked uncomfortable. "Let's stick to business. What about those two girls you have in your house?"

"You mean Marge and Belle? Why, what about them?"

"I'm asking you, lady. Don't you ask me. We have reason to believe they're operating—you know, hustlers. Coupla complaints have come in."

"Aren't you ashamed to come around spying on two young ladies? It so happens they are working girls, secretaries over in New York." And, with one of her strokes of imagination, added, "What's more, the pretty one, Marge, happens to be engaged."

The man regarded her silently for a moment. He didn't have a chance, and I felt sorry for him. "All right, ma'am, if that's all you gotta say. But tell 'em to be careful. We have an eye on 'em. And if you don't want to be an accessory, you be careful, too. A word to the wise." He turned to go, accidentally stumbled into the shower room, backed out again, found the door, and warily left.

My mother said to me, "They're wrong. The world is full of evil men. You mustn't believe them."

"Is Marge really engaged to be married?" I asked.

She pondered the question briefly. "Every girl is engaged to be married. It's a question of the right man finding her. Everybody is searching for the right person all the time. The lucky ones find each other."

"You mean I'm searching for someone right now?"

"Every minute," she murmured. "Now here's twenty cents. Go get yourself a hot lunch down the corner. A boy should have one hot meal a day."

I ran off, excited by the idea that, unknown to myself, I was searching for the right person. Was that the yearning I felt, unable to sleep on a warm night, hearing the ring of the High Striker bell on the avenue, or hearing the scream of the girl on the roller coaster being kissed all the way down the dizzying slide?

Yes. *It's love love love* . . . what else?

Within a week, a police wagon drove up. Two men entered our house. They apparently caught someone in the room who turned out to be a cop. It was a raid, and the neighbors came out of their houses as though it were a fire. Well, it was as good as a fire, I guess. The girls were screaming at the cops. My mother was indignant. She said to the driver, "They're not bothering anybody. Who are they bothering?" The onlookers heckled the cops. The red-haired neighbor who used to shout at my grandmother for spitting on the sidewalk, pointed to my mother. "Arrest her, she's the madame!" They rushed at one another, but were quickly separated. The police van roared off into the night with Marge and Belle. My mother shook her fist at the cops. "Who are they hurting? They are two lonely girls."

"What's your cut?" yelled redhead.

"You witch," retorted my mother. "May you grow bald overnight!"

Someone tossed a firecracker. The crowd scattered, it was an embarrassing evening.

My mother never wavered. The next day, she phoned the station house where the girls were kept, found out there was to be a hearing before a magistrate, and said she'd be there. She was appearing, she told my astonished father, as a character witness. And, wearing a gaily colored housedress, she sallied forth to meet the law.

Several hours later, she returned with a victorious smile, and with the two girls grinning sheepishly behind her. She had persuaded the judge to put them on probation in her custody.

She told them, seated on the bench, all three of them eating ice-cream cones, that they would have to change their lives. "You can't have too many friends in your room anymore. You, Marge, will go out and get a job. And Belle can work in the lockers where so many nice boys come." They nodded. But it didn't turn out that way, not exactly. The girls skipped before the week ended. My mother was heartbroken. She shook her head sadly. "I don't understand it, I don't understand it."

My father was gleeful. "You and your reforming schemes. Now watch them get into trouble and the police will arrest you this time."

"You'd like that, of course," she replied icily. "You'd like to see me behind bars, on bread and water."

"Just behind bars would be enough," said my father.

One bright morning, in walked Marge, a little less rouged, a little more modestly clothed, accompanied by a slightly balding, genial heavyweight.

"Hello," said Marge with a timid smile. My mother dropped her broom; they embraced tearfully. "This is Mickey, my husband," she said, taking Mickey's arm.

"Very pleased to meetcha," said Mickey, straightening his tie. "Marge has told me alla stuff about you."

"You got married," my mother exclaimed, "isn't that nice!"

"Yeah," said Marge. "I met Mickey at a bar one night last week, and we knew we was for each other. He has a good job, too." Mickey nodded importantly. Marge continued, "What we came by for, is to find out if you have a room for us to stay. We're sort of looking to set up house."

My mother clapped her hands. "I do have a room, just one, with a view, perfect for honeymooning!" She placed her arm around Marge's shoulder and led her into the hallway. Mickey dutifully followed.

My father doubted if they were married, but my mother was ecstatic, as if some mystery of the universe had been verified. "You see," she confided to me later, "they were searching for each other, two lonely people, and found each other. It's what life is all about."

About the other girl, Belle, we never heard anything.

∽ 10 ∽

The boardwalk fronted the ocean for miles. On many days I would lean against the iron railing, warmed by the sun, my eyes closed, listening to the sound of shoes. Sharp and muffled, quick and measured, clean-stepping and draggy, they moved over the boards, scuffing the surface, chipping it, smoothing it, wearing it down. And then, the resilient echo of the new boards laid in like bars of fresh linoleum, replacing the ones considered too dangerous. I could tell (just by listening) where the new boards were. A strange rhythm, a steady chatter, a lullaby. And I would fall asleep against the rail, for minutes at a time, then snap awake to the shoes again, the sound now a roar. I liked the sound. Thundering hoofbeats across the prairie! Stampede! Hide behind a rock, here they come!

I thrilled to the cowboy movies which had at least one good cattle stampede. I was a good judge of stampedes, especially on the sound part. If the sound scared you, it was a successful stampede. With a mass of people, the sound was just as deep, as rumbling, but you knew they were people and it didn't bother you. And it was different listening with eyes open or shut. I tried it both ways, deciding that eyes shut was the better way. I probably had my eyes shut for a year, maybe more, if you add up all the hours I listened on the boardwalk.

It was a world of blinding light, sharp air, and dense humanity.

Toward evening, a new sound: the footsteps changing from the easy stroller to the energetic stride of the seeker. The boardwalk lights came on. The ocean gleamed with a pale receding light, figures on the beach were slowly sheathed in darkness. Shouts like birdcalls filled the air. The last of the surf casters reeled in their lines. A few remaining kites of orange and blue caught the dying sun, while a strange moon appeared at the horizon as though put there by a magician. Boys and girls spread their blankets on the sand. The air was still warm. Music leaped out from unseen corners. Soon the boardwalk became a shimmer of light that spilled over onto the beach.

Under the boardwalk, enormous shadows deepened into pockets of darkness. I didn't go there often at night. We heard lots of stories of cops chasing boys and girls, sailors especially.

One night, as I started up the ramp to the boardwalk, a sailor whistled at me. I walked over. "You want to make an easy quarter, kid?" he asked.

A quarter! That was two frankfurters, one bag of potato chips, one root beer, and one corn on the cob. Or one frank, two chips, two roots. Or three chips, one root, one corn. Or something wild, one root and four corns!

"What do I do?" I asked eagerly. Jimmy Berkowitz edged up beside me, looking arrogant which was his natural peaceful look.

The sailor turned. I followed his glance and saw a bare-necked, short-skirted girl standing in the shadows near a concrete pillar. He said, "Here's what you do, you stay here and watch out for the cops. If you see a cop coming, just whistle. Can you whistle?"

"I can whistle," said Jimmy, and he did, almost blowing my ear off.

The sailor nodded. "That's all you do. OK?"

"When do I get the quarter?" I asked, recalling my mother's repeated admonition that if you don't ask you don't get anything in life. He hesitated, then reached into his pocket for the coin. "Now don't go away, or I'll find you and beat your ass off." I started to reply, but he continued, "I want you kids to stay here for one hour. Is that a deal?"

I nodded, so did Jimmy. The sailor left, and soon he and the girl disappeared under the boardwalk.

I tossed the quarter in the air, Jimmy snagged it, then he tossed it and I caught it and rolled it along the ground, he jumped on it and flipped it and caught it in his cap, all the time we were laughing like idiots.

It was getting dark now, very slowly because the ocean held the light longer than the land, and its reflection on the beach made it strangely undark, though you knew it was night. The darkness under the boardwalk was real, however. From that strip of sand came the strumming of guitars.

"There's gonna be a lot of nickels and dimes under there in the sand tomorrow," Jimmy ventured, rubbing his arms as the wind picked up with a flutter of cold air. "So what are we supposed to do now?"

86

"Watch for the cops," I said.

"Aah, you know there's no cops till late at night. Let's spend the money."

I didn't agree. We were paid to stand guard. Jimmy grumbled and said he'd get some soda pop for both of us. I gave him the quarter and he loped off, pretending to be lame on one foot.

"Don't be long," I called after him.

"Ha, ha, ho, ho, heh, heh, fongu Manchu!" His imitation Bela Lugosi laugh rolled back toward me. I wasn't worried. Jimmy was wild. It's true he stole empty milk and soda bottles and reclaimed the deposit pennies at the store. But he was honest considering all the lying that went on in the world.

I walked up and down like a soldier alert for enemy attack. The sounds from under the boardwalk floated out to me, and I tried to put them in some kind of order. The guitar was easy to isolate. The different laughters were harder. There were high ordinary laughs, then a lower kind of laugh, muffled, abrupt, often punctuated by giggling, or an oath. I walked over to the edge of the darkness and peered in. The overhead lights, small and dim, burned weakly through the faint mist. Now other voices reached my ears, softer, thicker. I heard a harsh breathing. I could see hurrying figures moving deeper into the darkness that was velvety and pure and throbbing with mystery.

Concrete pillars loomed, bodies leaning against them, bodies at the base, bodies on the sand, all embracing. I thought for an instant I saw the sailor but that face turned and vanished. A sour odor of sand, and another odor, heavy, human, exotic as spice, clung to my nostrils and excited me.

The guitar strummed idly. Nearby a sudden whispering arose in the dark, a woman's voice calling softly, urging, something about love, oh love me, love me, hold and love, ah love, my love, oh my darling, a sharp intake of breath joining hers, becoming a moan, a cry. Everywhere in the gray-black mist were the voices, low laughter, silence, then the guitar, and silence again. I was frightened. I understood the daytime, the lighttime, but here was too much of the unknown. I thought I heard a call for help, then silence, and the guitar singing O love I hold you O I kiss your lips . . .

I backed away from these shadows, and looked upward to the sky now icy with stars. The sharp air stabbed my lungs. I heard the sound of racing feet and Jimmy came into view, his tongue lolling out of his mouth, a bottle of soda in each hand.

"Where were you that long?" I cried out.

"Stealing soda," replied Jimmy. "I paid for one bottle and while he was getting change I snitched the other." We solemnly sat on the sidewalk and drank the soda. After a while, Jimmy asked, "How long we been here now?" It was half an hour, I figured. Jimmy said, "I'm hungry, let's get a frank and chips."

I shook my head. "We're supposed to guard the sailor."

"Guard him from what? He's been smooching under there long enough. I hope he gets the clap," Jimmy brayed like a jackass. I yodeled like a champion Swiss yodeler. The minutes passed. Not a single cop came by. The moon had moved way over to one side of the sky by now, and that takes some time, I thought, so the hour must have gone by. We agreed we had fulfilled our pledge, and raced straight under the boardwalk to the beach as though chased by demons. I flew the fifty yards through voices and whispers and laughter and that guitar. On the beach, we saw a turned-over lifeboat and in exhilaration galloped on and over it, our shoes ringing out a hollow tattoo on the curved ribbing. Then we picked up some seashells and hurled them against the boat. Suddenly, it lifted to one side, a man slipped out from under and scrambled toward us. Before I could turn and run, he had me by the leg. I howled in fear.

"Shut up, kid. Will you shut up?"

Jimmy was behind him, bellowing. "You let him go or I'll call a cop!"

The man faced Jimmy, his hands spread out in a gesture of conciliation. "Listen, you kids, be quiet. I'll make a deal with you. We got a little card game going on under the boat. We don't want no trouble with cops. Tell you what, if I give you a quarter, will you vanish, vamoose, go away, forget you saw this boat?" He looked pleadingly at us.

"OK," I said. "Cash in advance."

He flipped a coin and I seized it in midair, whirling with the same motion and running toward the boardwalk steps where the haven of light waited—the land of games, music, and people. Close behind, with a great whoop, Jimmy followed. The man, meanwhile, had lifted the overturned boat to slide back under, and my eye caught a flick of leg under the boat, a girl's leg, just as it settled back again on the sand. He had a girl there! Who else was there? More than two? Were they playing cards?

It didn't matter to us. Things were going on all the time, and nobody seemed to mind. Everybody was busy with what he wanted. Maybe that was the secret, to find out what it was you wanted to do. There were even people who paid you the same money for doing opposite things: a quarter for staying and a quarter for going away!

It didn't matter. We had forty cents left to spend, our mouths were watering. We joined the crowd on top of the boardwalk, happy to be in the light, moving our feet with the others in a sound louder to our ears than the surf coming in from the sea.

89

~ 11 ~

The house was set back from the street far enough to pro-
vide a moderate-sized flower garden. We hadn't planted
it, we just watched it grow. The grass came up in the
spring, then a few lilacs and roses, and soon these were
blighted or gone. By fall the twenty-by-twenty plot—
three feet above ground level—was littered with soda
bottles, rusty tin cans, condoms, corn on the cob, fruit
rind, tennis balls, and other assorted items of the passing
trade.

Still, the brief period of the roses lifted the spirit of
all. It was our only visible sign of Nature on the street:
not a tree, not a blade of grass, nothing green but the
small elevated mound in front of our house. Neighbors
would walk by on a mild evening to inhale the fragrance.

Once Mr. Perl clipped several roses, and my mother turned the water hose on him for a whole week whenever he passed by until he apologized.

My mother loved the roses; she shooed away dogs and cats and picked bugs off the leaves. Sitting on the bench during those evenings, she would turn to my father and ask, "Do you smell the roses?"

"Yes," he replied.

"Go up and smell them."

"I can smell them from here." My father never said more than he had to say on any subject. Right now, I could tell, he was enjoying the roses, happy they were part of the house.

My mother turned to me. "Breathe in and smell the roses."

"Yes, Momma."

"Is your nose clean?"

"Yes."

She took a deep deliberate breath. "God put roses on the earth to remind people of beauty. And He put them near our house because He knew we would appreciate them." My sister and I nodded but we didn't believe a word she said, because we knew she didn't believe in God, and was making the whole thing up. I was hoping my father would answer her, and he did.

"We had a tree in the back, but you cut it down," he said tartly.

"It was a sick tree," my mother replied.

My father continued as if she had not spoken. "You brought a man to cut it down."

"I can't stand suffering," she said, her voice rising. "And the tree was suffering."

"I liked that tree," my sister intruded timidly.

My mother turned on her. "Nobody asked you!" There was a silence. We watched the people go by. Our street

91

was crowded; it led directly to the beach and boardwalk a block away, whereas the street on either side ended at the avenue. Late in the evening, people used our street to funnel back from the boardwalk and out into other avenues and streets. You could hear them from inside the house, at the window, their footsteps scratching along the sidewalk. Sometimes, a fresh kid or a drunk would leap onto our garden and run off, the noise waking me.

My mother watched the people more and more. She would sit on the bench outside the house in the afternoon, her eyes half-closed, but her mind (I could tell) racing along. Whenever she was thinking about something, she would listen to you harder; it was a sign she was not really listening to you but to herself. For weeks she watched the people going thickly past our house.

Then one day she stopped thinking. She decided that our little flower garden would have to come to an end.

Why? How?

The why was simple: the plot of ground was going to waste. In that space there existed great commercial possibilities. Those people streaming by every day and evening—did it occur to us that they might be in need of refreshments or cigarettes?

Flash of lightning: a STORE!

The how was simple too: a power shovel drove up one morning, scoop and roar and clank, the elevation vanished, and a fresh floor of earth created level with the sidewalk. Then a carpenter arrived to construct plywood walls, a glass-encased counter, and finally an overhead X of beams over which a heavy tarpaulin was hung for a roof.

We were all unhappy. My sister and I felt bad about the roses being gone, we realized, forever. It changed the house, it was going to change everything. My father, one night at dinner, proclaimed, "She's finally going crazy." My mother pretended not to hear. She was called crazy so many times by her neighbors that it meant nothing to her. She may even have taken it as a compliment.

We worked hard to get the store ready. The whole idea depressed me. "Gee, it's terrible, Ma," I said as I tested the canvas roped around the upright posts.

She brushed away my remark. "Why is it terrible? It will bring in an income. There is nothing wrong—"

"I'm ashamed, if you want to know."

She laughed. "A store is fun. It's like a game. People stop by for soda or ice cream, you talk and learn to get along with strangers. It prepares you for life."

"If you want to know," I went on, "I hate the idea of standing behind a counter, with people watching me all the time." I turned away. "And I miss the roses."

"You miss the roses, do you?" Now her voice was brisk and angry. "Life isn't all roses, please remember. If you want roses, go to the park, the Botanical Gardens, there's miles of flowers. You can smell whenever you want. We won't talk about it any longer. You'll work in the store with your sister."

"I won't!"

"You will!"

Two days later, I was in the store—if you could call it that. It was like the trenches in the movie *All Quiet on the Western Front* with Lew Ayres. The water would seep in after a rain, and the earth would swell and rise up and sometimes cover the wooden slats that served as a floor. My sister and I caught colds.

At night, under the canvas, with a string of blinding light bulbs overhead, I served soda pop, flavored ices, cigarettes, ice-cream sodas and cones. The bulbs attracted an army of moths flickering wildly across the counter and very often into the open ice-cream cans. Many a moth would come up with a scoop of vanilla, and more than one was imbedded in the scoop unknown to myself or the customer.

People streamed by and clustered around the store making their small purchases. My mother sat on the bench enjoying it all while I hated it more every day. I even began to hate the ice cream, though I could eat all I wanted. At first, scooping the ice cream out of the cans was fun, but soon the moths (and sometimes roaches, once even a mouse) spoiled it for me. I got tired of making change, which in the beginning I enjoyed.

I knew we couldn't make much money running a dinky old store (which was really an open booth you took in every night along with the merchandise) but it didn't matter to my mother. What mattered was that our family was branching out in business—we also had the bath lockers—and most important our house was all lit up at night with the huge unshaded bulbs, an oasis in the dark street, a place for the last straggler to pause for a moment and rest or maybe buy a soda pop.

I guess in a week I opened a thousand soda pop bottles, and scooped out hundreds of ice-cream balls. And each day I was unhappier than the last. I dreaded having to stand in full view of the world. The customers called me Kid and Charlie and Jack and Boy and Dopey. My best friend Jimmy sneered at my white jacket (my mother insisted on a uniform). But mostly it was something inside me: I did not like to sell anything, to take money and give back money and count money. My mother liked to do all those things, it was a game. She'd count the pennies, nickels, dimes, and quarters like a child, stacking them in little piles, then wearily give it up and turn to something else. She lost money all the time, misplaced it, hid it and then couldn't find it, she even gave it away to beggars and strangers.

One day I awoke with a sore throat that lasted for a

week. My sister and mother took turns at the store, but when I was better I refused to go back. I kept making excuses. My mother begged and threatened. I was adamant. I wouldn't go back to the vanilla and chocolate cans and those crazy moths.

Then my mother said to me, "I'll get you a small radio. All for yourself. You won't have to let anyone else listen!" My heart quickened. A radio! We had a big radio in the living room with a lot of knobs that squealed most of the time—but a radio for myself . . . !

"When do I get it?" I asked.

"When you go back to the store. You can keep it in the store, right next to you, and play it as much as you like." She was tricky, all right. Jimmy had a crystal set with earphones, and we used to spend hours after school tuning in the squeals and once in a while the cat's whisker would find a real voice! But a radio that you plugged in and could carry anywhere you went, that was heaven. I knew sooner or later—at least until school started—I'd be back in the store, so I figured this way I'd get the radio.

It was a small buzzy box. I wouldn't let anyone borrow it, not Jimmy, not my sister, not even when my sister cried to hear Guy Lombardo or someone like that. My mother had to say it was my radio, that was that. I enjoyed making her take my part.

I kept the radio in the store, on a shelf next to my ear, while I batted away the moths, scooped the ice cream, opened bottle caps, and reached nimbly for cigarettes and candy. All day the radio chatted at my ear: talk, baseball, Benny Goodman, Russ Columbo, quiz shows. Sometimes my sister would listen after her work hours, and I didn't mind. As long as the radio was where *I* was, as long as she came to *me*.

One evening, after a rain, I sat alone in the store. It

was past eleven, and we closed at midnight. I wanted to close earlier this night because no one was out, even the moths stayed away, but my mother explained to me that the important thing about any business is reliability. The customer depended on a store being open, or a bank, or a train running on time. If the store hours ended at midnight, you couldn't close a minute earlier, she warned. In that one minute you could lose a best customer. Even the Telephone Company, she argued, with millions, tried to please every single customer.

I shivered in my thin sweater, not understanding how our store had anything to do with the Telephone Company. "It's the same principle," she continued, answering my unspoken question. "A customer who needs one cigarette is the same as a man who must make one phone call. You are learning how the world goes. This store is the world, remember that!" She left with a warning: "Not a minute before midnight!"

There was no baseball game, and some guy with bad tonsils was singing, so I turned the dial. My fingers caught a faint edge of music. I carefully tuned it in, bringing it closer. Still distant, the music was different from anything I heard in my life. It was strange and soft and silvery. It didn't go poom-poom like a popular song, it went more like pa-toom-la, toom-la, boom-a-ling toom toom, then repeated loud, then soft. The violins were all together, and I heard other strings throbbing, then they skipped rope together, and the melody (I don't know how) went through me like a delicious chill. I had never felt like that before. I wanted to hear it forever. Nobody ever played such music in the house.

It went on for two or three minutes, and I floated away in the sky, I floated past the fat light bulbs into the rainy night over Steeplechase, light as a thistle, while inside me something rose and fell with the music, as if I were part of the music, breathing it in and out, until I got a little dizzy and my heart rippled.

The music stopped. The voice on the radio said, "You have just listened to a performance of *Eine kleine*—" when a roll of thunder went through the sky and through the set. The voice came in clear again, ". . . will hear next a new work especially commissioned . . ." but I wasn't listening. My ear, my head, my heart, still held an echo. I must have dozed off with the rhythm of that music; then I heard my mother's voice calling from the back: "It's after midnight. Close up and put out the lights. Lights cost money!"

I fell asleep that night with a sense of discovery. What did "Eine kleine" mean? It was something foreign, I knew that.

Early next morning I asked my grandfather, who was also foreign, "What is Eine kleine?"

He looked up from his paper, startled. "Are you learning this in school?"

"No, Grandpa," I said. "It was over the radio."

"You heard this over the radio? It means a little thing . . . kleine."

I shook my head. "But it was about music." My grandfather brushed me away with a weary gesture and went back to his paper. It made no sense to him. But I had to find the answer. Who to ask? Mr. Hendler!

Mr. Hendler lived two houses away. He was a violinist and played at neighborhood weddings, and also he was sort of foreign though I wasn't sure which country. He was a friendly man. I dashed over to see him, and he invited me in.

"Sit down, my dear boy," said Mr. Hendler. He always spoke like that: my dear boy, my dear friend, my dear woman. He wore a neat summer suit and a little blue bow tie. "Sit down, we'll talk, my young friend," he said, and he sat down himself on a tattered hassock.

"Excuse me, Mr. Hendler, I have a question—"

"And I promise to answer it, you can be sure!"

I nodded. Maybe he would, he was an educated man and played the violin. Except for my music teacher in school, he was the best person to ask a music question. His friendly eyes blinked behind his skinny glasses. "Your question, may I ask? Is it about arithmetic, or spelling?"

"No." I spoke with difficulty. "It's about music. Not jazz but real music. You know, the other kind . . ." I hesitated. "What they play with a conductor."

"Perhaps you mean classical music," he suggested.

"What you play on the violin!" I blurted out. I was silent for a moment. Then I asked (he was waiting for me to speak), "What is Eine kleine? I heard the man say it over the radio."

He took off his glasses and laughed. "You mean, I'm sure, *Eine kleine Nachtmusik*. Nacht means Night. It means the kind of music for Nighttime. Little Night Music. Very wonderful."

I asked, "Who wrote it?"

"Mozart."

"Who is Mozart?"

"No, no, not with a *z*, with a *ts*, like this, *Mo–tsart*." Mr. Hendler was patient, and careful.

"Who is he?"

"He is God," answered Mr. Hendler, in a hushed voice. "If not God, the closest to God." And he got up from the hassock, went to the closet and brought out a violin.

"Mozart," he said quietly. And he played a music not exactly what I heard on the radio, but the same kind. Again, it took hold of me with a throbbing joy, as though the music came from me, I became the violin almost! He played for a minute or more, then stopped very gracefully—you knew the selection was over—and lifted his bow, and said in that same voice the one word "Mozart."

I nodded, thanked him, and went out. I hurried to the corner library and looked into an encyclopedia. I turned the pages to M, and then Ma, Mi, Mo . . . "Mozart, Wolfgang Amadeus. 1756–1791. Austrian composer."

That was him! The man Mr. Hendler called God. Wolfgang Amadeus Mozart. I ran back home to help open the store, repeating the full name over and over to myself like a magic charm. When I reached the house I asked my sister in a triumphant voice, "Take three guesses. Who's Wolfgang Amadeus Mozart?"

"Who's *what*?" she giggled.

"He wrote *Eine kleine Nachtmusik,* you dope." I pulled one corner of the canvas down to let the night's rainwater run off. Just then my mother came out of the house carrying the bag of coins to start the day's business. She glanced at the clearing sky and chanted, "After the rain comes sunshine. The store is the world, my children!"

~ 12 ~

Grandfather didn't enter the living room, he made an entrance. It was part of the general importance he gave to himself. He wanted you to know this was no ordinary caller, but the patriarchal fount, the top man of the family tree; as though, flowering above the gnarled branches, he gave the whole structure some dignity.

Coming up the street, briskly, erect, he walked with a reverence that somehow gave him an added height. He generally wore a neat black suit, black hat, and dark shoes to match. A heavy cane hung from his arm. He had a delicate way of stroking his beard with the back of his hand. His eyes were always alert, and in them lurked an ironic and disinterested smile.

On this day, as always, he knocked on the door sharply with his cane, thrust it open, and stood framed in the doorway. He coughed lightly, sucked through his teeth and announced, "I'm here!"

On this day, as always, my mother called out the same warning, "Watch the step!" And Grandfather, with a re-assuring wave of his hand, casually stepped down. He had become quite used to the sharp drop into the room, but he enjoyed my mother's alarm.

The room was easily a foot and a half below the street level; it was once part of a basement that had been con-verted into a "downstairs" apartment for the summer. Having stepped down, he came forward and kissed my mother on the cheek. "How are you today, Daughter?" he asked. He then turned and patted my head. "How is your grandma?"

"She's all right," I said. "I talk to her every day."

"You mean she talks to *you* every day." He winked and clucked his tongue. "I'll go in and see her, then we'll have a cup of tea." He left his hat on the chair and walked through the door to Grandmother's room in the rear of the house.

After a few minutes, he returned. "She's fine, with God's help," he said absently. "She looks fine."

"Wouldn't you like her to move back with you?" my mother asked.

Grandfather shook his head firmly. "No. You can take care of her better. A mother who is ill belongs with the daughter." As if to end the subject, he began to sip the tea which my mother had placed on the table. He bit into a cube of sugar and nodded in my direction. "Well, little scholar, how is school?"

"There's no school in the summer, Grandpa."

"Ah . . ."

"It's vacation. Nobody does nothing."

"So what's in your head during the summer, cream cheese?"

"Nothing, Grandpa. I just play ball and swim."

"Why don't you go to the synagogue?"

"Gosh, there's nothing to do there."

"What's gosh? What word is gosh? Look at you, you're growing up, not a Jewish word in your head." He sneezed violently, rearranged his beard, and waved a finger at me.

I said, "I don't believe in God, Grandpa."

He bristled, but kept his poise. "God cares whether you believe or not? Go wipe your nose." He drummed on the chair with his fingers. "No wonder the boy lives without the Lord in his heart. Look at his father. Not even on the High Holy Days is he in the synagogue!" He made a clicking noise with his teeth.

"When he gets a little older, he'll believe," my mother said.

Grandfather was silent, his eyes closed, his head cocked slightly to one side. He was asleep.

My mother cautioned for me to be silent. I sat on the stool watching him breathe with a soft rasp, his hands folded across his lap. Grandfather had a habit of abruptly dozing off and just as abruptly waking again. Once he fell asleep in the middle of a long sentence, and as we started to tiptoe out, he gave a slight shudder, opened his eyes, and completed the sentence. No one dared walk out on him.

I watched his face tranquil in sleep, a flicker of a smile caught at the corner of his mouth. He seemed the picture of innocence. And yet rumors constantly crackled about him. Was it true, I wondered, that he moonshined some high-proof sacramental wine in the basement of the synagogue? And what of the talk that he molested several astonished grandmothers in the balcony during services? Did he, as some claimed, take a quick swig of liquid before sundown on the Day of Atonement, when neither bread nor water was to touch the lips of the believer? And a certain Mr. Lerner, who hated him, being of a reformed sect, giggled it about that he had seen Grandfather leaving a burlesque house. But Grandfather came through rumor and character assassination with full sail.

His eyes opened. "With such a father, what do you expect of the boy?" He spoke as though he had not slept. "But I've said it before, nobody listens." Whereupon he turned to me with his favorite subject. "I will live to a hundred. And why will I live to be a hundred, little scholar? First, I ask it humbly of the Lord. Second, I watch my digestion. A hot glass of water before breakfast. That's the secret. One hot glass of water, every morning for sixty-five years!" He winked. "If I could sell bottles of hot water, I'd be rich. People would drink it from bottles. From a glass they don't drink."

He asked again about each member of the family, soberly offered advice, then rose from the chair.

My mother said, "Take a taxi, Poppa."

Grandfather stiffened. "Little daughter, I am no cripple. These legs were given to me by the Lord, and they will carry me wherever I have to go." He walked to the door.

"Be careful going up," said my mother.

"Going up, going down," he grumbled in reply. "I've been coming here long enough to know." He stepped up, opened the door, and pointed his finger at me. "You don't believe in God? See if God will worry!" I wanted to laugh whenever he pointed his finger at me, but I liked him too much to laugh while he was in the house.

As soon as he walked out, I began to laugh. My mother said sharply, "Go after him and apologize."

"But I didn't say anything bad."

"Go on!"

"But I don't believe in God."

"Tell him you're sorry, even if you have to lie."

I ran into the street and caught up with Grandfather. "I'm sorry, Grandpa."

"For what are you sorry?" He stopped, smacking his lips.

"I think maybe God is really there," I mumbled.

"He cares what you think?" Grandfather's voice was edged with scorn. "He has enough to worry about."

"Does God forgive, Grandpa?"

"Of course He forgives."

"Then He'll forgive me for not being sure if I believe. If I'm wrong, he'll forgive me," I said.

His eyes twinkled. "You little *momser*. Go swim. But if you're in the water, and you start to drown, remember to call out to God. He will give you strength. But why should He hear you if you don't believe in Him? I'll tell you why. Because I pray for all of you. He respects the head of the family. So go, swim, here's five cents, buy ice cream."

I took the money and shouted as I ran off. "Thanks. Come visit us again!"

He marched off, head and shoulders erect.

That night, at dinner, my mother brought up the subject. Turning to my father, she said, "I'm worried about that step for Poppa."

"What step?" he asked.

"The step going down. One day he'll fall."

"He won't fall. He's going to live to be a hundred. Didn't you hear him say so?" His voice was heavy with mockery.

"It's very dangerous when you come into the house." My mother began slicing an apple. "It's a big drop from the street door."

My father sipped his coffee, he thought for a moment.

"I can't lift up the room and make it even with the street."

"You can put in a step."

"He's been coming in fine up to now. I don't want a step sticking out into the room. He gets down fine. I've watched him. He can do it without looking." My father indicated by his tone that he considered the matter closed.

But a week later the subject came up again. I could hear their voices flaring up through the wall of the bedroom.

"Will you stop that?" my father said. "Now stop nagging me."

"I want a step for my father," my mother retorted.

"There is nothing wrong with your father!"

"He's getting old."

"He has pink cheeks, he'll never grow old."

"I'm ashamed that he can't go upstairs or downstairs like a human being. He has to step into a hole."

I heard a loud sigh. "He's used to that, he knows just how to step down."

Now her voice rose higher. "You hate him, don't you? You must hate him!"

"I don't—"

"You want to see him get killed. You'll laugh at that poor man's funeral. In your heart you're cruel. You have no consideration for old age."

"I will not build a step."

My mother demanded, "You have a hammer and nails and lumber. Build *something*!"

A week went by. Then, unannounced, Grandfather knocked on the door with his cane, thrust it open and stepped briskly down. "Watch out," called my mother, but he was already down, below (as we used to call it) sea level. He sneezed, smoothed out his beard, and said, "I want to go over my insurance."

"What's the matter?" My mother was alarmed.

"Nothing is the matter."

"Sit down and have some tea."

"I won't sit today. I'll be back after the Sabbath. Please tell my sons to be here, ten o'clock."

"What for, Poppa?"

"My insurance. Are you deaf? I want to go over the policies. Phone Ralph to bring them."

I called out from the next room. "Hi, Grandpa!"

He ambled to the door. "Hi, gosh, gee whiz . . . such words in your head! A prayer you haven't got, not one, eh?"

"I prayed yesterday, honest I did."

"Where did you pray, Spinoza?"

"In the water. I swam out too far and lost my breath and swallowed water, and then I prayed."

"And someone saved you?"

"I was near the rope, and I grabbed onto it."

His head nodded. "Who made you reach out and grab the rope? God."

"Yes, Grandpa," I said, knowing it had pleased him, even though I knew in my heart I had grabbed the rope only because Jimmy pushed me on it.

"I will live to a ripe old age, and there is one reason only." Whereupon he lifted his finger heavenward as though the gesture made any further discussion superfluous, and stepped out into the bright air. I heard him whistling at the birds as he walked away.

The day before the Sabbath, my mother softly pleaded with my father for a step going down. He listened stonily. "Not so much for myself, but my brothers are coming tomorrow. I don't want anything bad to happen."

"I will not build a step," he said. "I'll do something, but not a step."

The next morning my father constructed a little ramp descending into the room. It was smoothly fitted against the door base, and sloped in a gradual incline to the floor. I tried it out by going up and down the ramp a dozen times. My mother was pleased. "He'll love it. I know he'll love it," she murmured. "And it will be much easier for him."

The day arrived, and the night of what was to be Grandfather's last visit. Two of my uncles had arrived half an hour earlier, a little uneasy about the subject their father chose to discuss. They were beneficiaries of his insurance, and feared perhaps a sudden whimsical change in the old man's mind that would make them beneficiaries no longer. Uncle Ralph fidgeted in his chair. He drank his cup of tea in silence. Uncle Morty kept snorting and throwing out alarming thoughts. "He's going crazy, the Old One. No, he's there already. Maybe he'll make God the beneficiary."

"Shut up," said Uncle Ralph.

"Who's giving orders?" sneered Uncle Morty.

"Quiet, please," implored my mother. "I don't want any fighting when he comes."

Uncle Ralph's cigar went out. They all sat there waiting for the Old One to enter, except my father who stayed away from family conferences. I wondered what Grandfather was going to do. A strange feeling grew inside me that this evening was not to end in any ordinary fashion. I imagined an argument, complete with loud threats and fainting (my mother always fainted on these occasions), topped off with Grandfather storming from the room with a leap upward at the door. I had witnessed this once before, in a movie, except instead of Grandfather with a beard it was Douglas Fairbanks with a shining sword.

While we waited, Grandfather was briskly approaching the house. And here Fate was preparing a most unusual end. Was it Fate that prickled the flesh at the back of my neck, caused me slowly to rise, and quickened my breathing? Fate was what waited for you. It was never good or bad. It was what waited and had to happen. Suddenly I felt with a pang that it was about to happen to this man with the heavy hands and twinkling eye.

His footstep was at the door. His cane knocked. The door swung open.

"Watch out!" I cried.

It was an old familiar warning for Grandfather, though a startled look crossed his face as he realized it was my voice that spoke the words. With the ease of all his previous entrances, and his head held high, he stepped down into the room. But instead of the accustomed space, his bending leg touched the unfamiliar ramp. His knee buckled. With a gasp, he fell.

My mother shrieked. My uncles sat stunned. My father ran in.

He had broken his hip. Five days later he died from complications which included pneumonia.

For months my mother bitterly accused my father of plotting a murder, while my father blamed the whole idea on my mother.

Grandfather, body and soul, had trundled off to heaven. One question kept humming through my mind, day and night, over and over: "If he was so close to God, why didn't God warn him? Why?"

∾ 13 ∾

People moved in and out of our house all the time. I had to do a lot of extra work, such as removing small beds from some rooms and replacing them with larger beds, or the other way around. I became an expert on beds, how to fold them, carry them, how to take them apart, how to clean them and repaint them. Cleaning a bed for the summer trade was very important. The heat and dampness and crowding increased the bedbug population; you cleaned a bed one week and there they were again a week later—bedbugs by the hundreds, thousands, maybe millions if you counted all the beds in our house. They lived mostly in the four corner posts and joints; also, they liked bedsprings.

Killing bedbugs looked easy, but it wasn't. Most people used sprays and kerosene. In our house, we burned them. I would take the bed apart, carry out the sections in the alleyway, light up a folded newspaper and hold it to the corner joints. Or sometimes (with my father's permission) I would use a blowtorch, which was most exciting of all. It roared with a blue and orange flame as I would sweep it along the iron, catching the bedbugs before they could run. I killed millions of them. I was a cool killer. It was like a machine gun in the movies, in my ears the blowtorch went rat-a-tat-tat, the blue and orange bullets never missing as the bugs fell to the pavement. My sister would stand off and watch, frightened, from the open garage, hiding behind Grandmother's chair.

"He's burning the bugs. He's burning them!" she cried.

And Grandmother chanted, "Where is he? What is he doing? Who is he burning? He's a monster, that boy! One day he'll burn your father." And she cackled and coughed with delight.

One tenant, we called him Frank, liked to watch me work. He sat on a little canvas chair which he moved around to catch the sun. Sitting on his chair, a dirty toothpick hung between his teeth, as I cleaned or painted the beds, he would say, "Good work, kid. That's how to do it. You know how to do it," his face in a twisted grin. I didn't like Frank. He was sort of old, older than my father, and with a narrow almost deformed body. He seemed to slide sideways when he walked, as though trying to hide his body. His shirt was always dirty. We never found out anything about him, and my mother never inquired. "If people won't talk," she once told me, "they have nothing to say."

My father rarely commented on the tenants, he accepted them as a fact of life. He never said a word to

Frank, and once he said to me, as we passed Frank in the hallway, "There's another bedbug."

Jimmy Berkowitz thought Frank was a gangster on the lam. For example, he pointed out that Frank seldom left the house or its vicinity during the day, a sure sign he was hiding out. "And he don't look you in the eye, you notice?" added Jimmy. "Wouldn't surprise me if he packs a rod."

Frank lived alone in a rear upstairs corner room which faced a row of backyards hung with wash most of the time. One day he brought his daughter to live with him. That meant he was married and was once part of a family, and if he was really a gangster maybe he stole to support his family. The daughter was a thin, fair-skinned girl of about seventeen, with large eyes. We didn't see her very much. She was in her room most of the time, except when she went out for a walk with Frank.

My sister and I tried to make friends with her. She was shy, and didn't speak too well or clearly. I tried to make her smile by telling her jokes. Frank was always near her. He seemed to be watching her, especially when she sat in the alleyway getting some sun. I thought she was pretty. My mother thought she had tuberculosis or something because no matter how long she sat in the sun she was always pale. She never cared to come into our living room and listen to the radio. She was embarrassed when I asked her, and turned to Frank.

"How do you feel, dear?" he asked.

"I have a headache," she replied, looking at the ground, her hand pushing her hair back over her forehead.

"Then you better go upstairs and rest." She nodded and quietly went into the house. Frank explained, "She lost her mother a year ago, and has a lot of headaches." It was a funny way to explain a headache, I thought. Sometimes I wouldn't see her for a week at a time, and when I asked Frank how she was feeling, he replied gruffly, "She's all right. She don't like the sunshine, so she stays indoors."

Once, sitting outside on the bench, she smiled at me. It was a wan, sad smile. Then she quickly turned away, picked up a magazine, and began to read silently to herself. I don't think I heard her speak more than five times during the first month she was in our house.

Frank also had two brothers whom he introduced to my mother. They were younger than he, and sometimes his brothers would go upstairs with him for hours, and sometimes one of them would take Carol (that was her name) out for a walk while her father would stay in the house with his other brother.

One afternoon, I was upstairs in the rear house to check on a leaking icebox. Passing Frank's door, I heard voices. I stopped to listen. He was talking, she answered, suddenly he shouted at her, then she was yelling at him, and their voices came through the door in wild disorder. I heard him say, "You little bitch, you're going to listen to me." Then her voice: "Don't talk to me like that!" A scream.

I knocked on the door. I didn't mean to, I knocked before I knew it, and withdrew my hand violently. I wanted to run, but couldn't. It got very quiet behind the door. Then it opened.

Frank regarded me coolly. "What is it, kid?"

Behind him I saw Carol at the window, looking out. She wore a robe hung loosely from her shoulders, her hair was uncombed, her feet bare. She looked swiftly in my direction, turned and walked to a chair. Her robe opened as she sat down, and my eye caught a flash of her nakedness.

112

"What is it, kid?" Frank repeated.

"The icebox. My mother said . . ." I stammered.

"Nothing's wrong with our icebox. You tell your mother." And he slowly closed the door.

I climbed the stairwell ladder to the roof, my mind churning. They seemed funny, something was funny in that room. The way she looked at him, then sat down and crossed her legs, she didn't seem to care what he said or thought. She was old enough not to listen to her father, I guess. Her swift glance in my direction . . . was there a faint smile on her lips? I couldn't remember for sure.

I lay on my back, on the roof pebbles, and looked up at the soft white clouds. Maybe I could become friends with Carol, even though she was older. We could go to the boardwalk and take in the rides. I closed my eyes and imagined we were white clouds chasing each other, gently moving across each other, floating side by side like dolphins, until it suddenly got dark, the wind increased, and a bolt of lightning stabbed out of me and struck her and she turned all flame . . . I opened my eyes lazily and spotted a whorl of pigeons over a distant roof. That's what I wanted to do: raise pigeons and train them to fly in circles and answer my signals when I called. And I wouldn't wave a flag on a stick, either; I would motion with my fingers like those deaf-and-dumb people on the beach. My pigeons would be very smart.

On my way down from the roof, as I descended the stairway, I heard a voice from the landing above. I looked up. It was Carol. "Hello," she called. "Would you do me a favor, please?" I nodded, staring at the buttons of her robe. "Would you get me a pack of smokes? Any kind." She tossed me a quarter.

"Does your father let you smoke?" I asked.

She laughed, a low, light laugh. "Oh, sure, kid. He lets me do lots of things. I'd appreciate it, just leave the pack outside the door. Keep the change."

I watched her disappear from the landing. My heart leaped with my footsteps dancing down the stairs.

That evening, after dinner, I asked my mother. "Who are they, anyway? Who is Frank?"

She looked up. "What do you mean, who is Frank? He's a tenant like all my other tenants."

"I wonder where he's from, or what he does."

"I don't ask my tenants questions," she said briskly. "If they pay their rent, they can stay. If not, out they go."

I swallowed, and said, "I brought Carol some cigarettes. She gave me a nickel."

My mother rose from the chair. "Did you finish painting the beds?"

"Yes."

"Go talk to your grandmother."

"I don't like to talk to her. She's crazy."

My mother raised a warning finger. "Don't say that!" She sighed. "Sometimes being crazy can be the best thing to happen to a person."

That night, I sneaked back upstairs, hoping I might see Carol and maybe run another errand for her. I walked down the hall, when suddenly I heard voices on the stairs. I hid in the hall closet. I heard Frank and Carol talking as they passed. I peeked out of the closet, then quickly pulled the door shut as other footsteps sounded on the stairs. I opened the door a chink to see another man follow them inside the room. He looked like one of Frank's brothers.

I crept out of the closet toward the closed door. Muffled voices, a man's hard laughter. A voice saying, "Let's go, kid." Someone (the brother?) said something about money. Carol answered, the words unclear. Frank now, violent: "I'll throw you out, you want to be out on the street?" Was it directed to Carol, or the brother . . . ? I heard a sharp sound, like a slap. "Let me go, you

114

bastard!" There was a scuffle, a chair overturned, a glass smashed to the floor. Then Carol wept, a low sobbing.

I ran down the stairs and into our living room. My mother was sorting linen, placing sheets and pillowcases into separate piles. I took a deep breath. "There's a fight upstairs!"

She put down the pillowcases. "Where?"

"In Frank's room. And there's another man . . . they're hurting her."

"How do you know?"

"I was listening at the door."

Her voice leaped out at me. "Why do you listen? It's none of your business what goes on behind anyone's door, you understand? Stay away from other people's doors!"

"But Carol was crying. Maybe we ought to call the cops."

"We are not calling the police. It's a family problem, every family has problems. Isn't it almost time for bed?" She closed her eyes, and swayed slightly. "Go on to bed."

For the first time I felt something different about her. She looked different to me, she was hiding something. I always used to believe what she said, but now I wasn't sure. Dark feelings whirled inside me.

"Go on to bed," she repeated softly, her face turned toward the window. I went out, hoping I'd see my father to tell him what happened. Did I dare talk to him behind my mother's back? The idea made me shiver. But my father was nowhere in sight.

Later, on the way to my room, I stopped at that door again. I put my ear against it. Silence inside. Were they all in bed, asleep? That other strange man . . . Then the thought rocked through my head: he wasn't Frank's brother. And Frank . . . he wasn't Carol's father!

I ached to save her. I wanted more than anything at

115

that moment to be grown-up and powerful. I'd smash down the door and grab Frank and his friend, one with each hand, and slowly choke them to death.

I hurried to my room down the hall. I undressed, trembling, and tried hard to sleep, but a voice inside me kept me awake. What was it like to be in bed with Carol? The image of her legs beneath her robe swept my mind like a flame. If I were older, right now, I could become friends with Frank, and he would let me . . . Overcome with shame, I lay agonized under the blanket. I was as bad as the others. I wanted her like the others. I felt sleep coming on, and asked it to hurry and save me from these thoughts. Swarming over me were the sounds and voices heard under the boardwalk, confused, mysterious, frightening, the guitar and whisper of love, shadows moving toward one another with kisses and silent embrace. It was a world that waited for all, not only on the beach but in rooms, in daylight or dark. A tide of desire rose under me and carried me into sleep.

The next morning, I awoke late. The sun was high at my window. I dressed, and hurried past Frank's door. It was slightly ajar. I pushed it open. The room was empty. Wooden hangers and shoe boxes lay scattered on the floor. A pair of silk stockings hung from a hook in the closet. Bureau drawers were open at crooked angles, a mirror was pulled off the wall with its hook.

My mother was alone in the kitchen. She looked up as I entered. "They're gone. I told Frank to leave. I don't like noisy tenants in my house." She paused, then asked, "Are you hungry? I cooked a cereal you like."

She was too nice to me. But I knew, and just to let her know, I didn't eat breakfast. I didn't eat all day.

~ 14 ~

After several weeks of trying to run our store, my mother gave up—that is, she gave up on my sister and me. "You haven't got the spirit," she admonished us. "Without spirit and imagination, you can never succeed in business." We agreed. And so, the store (O forgotten rose garden!) was rented to a Mr. Weber, and I became his errand-runner.

For some reason that I could never figure out, Mr. Weber credited me with more intelligence than I had. I was cheerful, maybe that was the reason. He was a pessimist. He sat outside on the bench and saw the future as a continual threat. Like all summer concessionaires, he was much concerned about the weather. He would look up at the cloudless sky and murmur, "Must it rain

117

on weekends?" That was his favorite expression.

Rainy weekends could mean the difference between a reasonable profit, breaking even, or a loss. And so the weather was watched, worried about, prayed for, and cursed. Of all the worriers, Mr. Weber worried hardest. He generally worried most when I was around. It got worse after Wednesday, because, with weather changing all the time, a bright Monday, Tuesday, and Wednesday could possibly mean a cloudy Thursday or Friday, which could then mean a rainy Saturday and Sunday, so if anyone was going to worry, it was too late to worry when the weekend came, you had to start earlier. And, being a real worrier, Mr. Weber always started early.

On the second Thursday in August, he said to me, "Well, what do you think for tomorrow? You think rain?"

"I don't think so, Mr. Weber," I replied with not too much enthusiasm.

"You don't know. Nobody knows," he sighed. "The radio says one thing, but you think the rain listens to the radio?" He laughed uneasily.

"Rain is caused by moisture and condensation," I said, hoping it would cheer him up somehow. "I don't feel any moisture today."

He looked at the cloudless sky, shaking his head. "It didn't rain too much in July. But last Sunday, it was August first, it rained. I'm worried about August. It's a bad sign that it rained the first Sunday in August."

"It was only in the afternoon, Mr. Weber," I said, trying again to reassure him.

And Mr. Weber, falling back on his favorite phrase, his ultimate appeal to fate, exclaimed, "Must it rain on weekends?" He gave me a ten-dollar bill to pick up several cartons of cigarettes and candy. "Don't lose the change," he warned.

I was glad to run errands for him; I got tired of just hearing all that weather talk.

The sky was clear on Friday, but Saturday brought a slow drizzling rain. The avenue was deserted, except for some hardy stragglers. Mr. Weber stood at the store window and looked out upon the wet street. I was drinking a milk shake. "Tomorrow will rain too, you'll see," he whispered. The rain ended that night; a mist hung over the spires and roller coasters; the hot dog and popcorn vendors sat moodily in their chairs, dreaming of Sunday and clear skies. The rain returned Sunday morning and lasted all day. On Monday, the sun broke through.

I knew how bad Mr. Weber was feeling so I didn't hang around the store on those rainy days. I couldn't bear to see his face when it rained on weekends. Also, he was always asking me questions as if I knew the answers. Couldn't he see I just went along with him?

On Monday I saw his wife coming up the street. Mrs. Weber was a small woman with gray hair and dark shadows under her eyes. Her lips were moving as she approached. She was worrying just like her husband, except he would groan out loud while she only moved her lips. Maybe there was another reason, but I couldn't figure it out. Maybe she was more scared than worried. I liked Mrs. Weber because she didn't talk too much. After an hour of my mother talking, it was nice to sit in the store and listen to Mrs. Weber who nodded, with her lips moving silently.

"Good morning," I said, and she stopped.

"And to you also," she replied in a sad, low voice.

"Where's your husband today?"

"Mr. Weber is in bed all day today, and also yesterday."

"Gee, I'm sorry to hear it," I said.

"He got sick yesterday in the morning. He looked out of the window, and when it began to rain, right away he got sick. My nephew is in the store today." She shook her head. "Why don't you stop in the house later and say hello? He likes company." With a nod, she walked past me on her way to the avenue.

I couldn't refuse Mrs. Weber. That evening, I rang their bell (they lived on our street) and Mr. Weber opened the door. I said I was glad to find him walking around. He shrugged his shoulders, "It's nothing . . . a man gets a cold, what's the excitement?" Mrs. Weber brought tea and crackers. "He didn't have a cold, he had a heartache, you know what I mean?" She nodded significantly. "He takes everything so serious. Look at him."

Mr. Weber scowled, "Why should he look at me? He don't see me enough in the store?" He grumbled, "There's three more weeks to the season, and she says I shouldn't be serious. Ask her how much money we made this summer. Ask her."

I gulped my tea. I didn't know why I should ask her anything. After all, she wasn't my mother. I didn't know if my mother would want me to visit her tenants and discuss business.

"He says ask me," she spoke, "but even if I said he was right, is that a reason to frighten me, to just go to bed and stare at the ceiling for two whole days?"

"How much rent do you pay?" I asked timidly.

"Enough," said Mr. Weber. "Too much."

"If you're in business, you pay rent," said Mrs. Weber firmly. "It's a question whether we should be in such a business."

I finished my tea as quickly as I could, before that question was discussed, mumbled good night, and left.

At home, I told my mother of my visit to the Webers, and about their troubles. When I brought up the rent, my mother frowned. "I can't reduce the rent, because I pay their rent to the mortgage company. He'll have to do the best he can."

"But if the weather is bad, is that his fault?" I asked.

"No, it's mine," she answered sharply.

"But Ma—"

"Mr. Weber can borrow if he can't make the last payment. Everybody borrows, that's why there are banks." My mother was very good-hearted although she pretended to be tough. I had seen her give up rent many times if she liked the particular tenant. Maybe she didn't like Mr. Weber. He *was* sort of a pest, I admit. Anyway, things got worse for him.

During the following week, he became morose and preoccupied. He was gruff with me. When I returned from one of my errands, he accused me of withholding some of the change. Soon after, he apologized. He watched the sky with apprehension. On Wednesday, it clouded over, then cleared, then clouded again on Thursday. "Good," he laughed nervously. "Let it rain all night. Plenty of moisture and . . . what else?"

"Condensation."

"Let there be both, today, tomorrow, plenty!"

"Yeah," I said. "After a big rain, Mr. Weber, comes clear skies. I read it in my science book in school."

But his prayers went unanswered. It seemed as if God were mocking him. The rain did not exhaust itself. It continued intermittently through Saturday and Sunday, wrecking the weekend business.

I heard, on Monday, that Mr. Weber was away, visiting a brother in New Jersey. But Mrs. Weber whispered to me while I was drinking a milk shake that he was at home, he wouldn't leave the house even though there was nothing wrong with him that she could see. "He sits listening to the radio all the time. He don't eat, he talks to himself." She wrung her hands. "He'll get a breakdown. I say every year, why do we need this business? But he likes the seashore, and we need something to do, and it isn't too hard work . . . but I don't like him to get a breakdown."

I didn't know what to say. "Are you sure you don't need more cigarettes or soda syrup, Mrs. Weber?" She clapped her hands, "Yes, I can see you know the business better than me. You should be in this business maybe!"

"My mother wanted me to," I replied. "But I fell asleep at the counter every day."

"No, no, that's no good." She laughed, and I did too. Then she said, "I'm worried about him. Laugh he won't, but if you could make him smile . . ."

On Thursday, his hair cut, with a clean white shirt, Mr. Weber appeared behind the counter. He began shining up the soda glasses and the milk shake containers. He cleaned the big mirror behind the soda fountain. And he called out to me again: "Well, my boy, how does it look? Tomorrow is another Friday. You're a smart boy, well? Yes or no?"

"The radio says favorable for the weekend," I said, hoping he would smile.

He leaned toward me, a snarl on his face. "The radio lies. They all lie!" He seized my arm, trembling, and released it quickly. "Excuse me. Did you ever hear such a thing? If the sun shines this next weekend, I have a happy winter. If it rains, misery. Did you ever see people should live this way?" He fumbled at a cigar, lit it, shook his head from side to side, winked at me, and said, "I'll go crazy, you'll see." And for a minute I thought maybe he was, already, because I had never seen him act that way. But when I thought of all the days of rain during August,

122

on the wrong days, and also in July, it was enough to get anyone crazy.

I kept thinking the next day, with the sun in and out of the clouds, how a person goes crazy. It would be funny if Mr. Weber suddenly said he was Napoleon, or something. Would they come and take him to the booby hatch? I tried to imagine what he would do. He was too peaceful a man to do much, I thought. Maybe some people just can't go crazy even if they wanted to. I didn't know how I would go crazy, for instance. Would I start laughing like Dr. Jekyll and Mr. Hyde? It was scary to think about.

Later that afternoon, everything started to happen like in one of those silent Charlie Chaplin movies, everything fast and jerky. Children playing on the street, people sitting in front of their houses—when suddenly there was a smashing of glass inside the store, and Mr. Weber emerged, holding a broken soda glass in his hand. He stood there, as if surprised at finding himself in that spot, looked dumbly at the glass and tossed it into the trash can. He breathed in with a gasp, and seemed to hold his breath. I thought for a minute he would scream. It looked like he was going to, but was gritting his teeth. His face was white, his eyes wild, his hands clenching and unclenching at his side.

I took a step toward him; he looked like a sleepwalker and I once read if you speak softly to a sleepwalker he'd wake up. I came over to him, touched his sleeve, and said, "Mr. Weber . . . ? It's me."

His face turned toward me but his eyes didn't see me. He strode abruptly from the sidewalk and lay down in the middle of the street, on his back. A car drew up, slowed, stopped. The driver poked his head out of the window. Mr. Weber raised his head from the pavement and shouted, "Come, run me over!" Then he lay back, and waved to the car to ride over him.

The driver opened the car door and came forward slowly. A crowd gathered. Mrs. Weber called from the sidewalk, weak with fear. "What are you doing? Get up. Do you hear me? Help him, somebody!" I ran into the street, through the grinning faces of the crowd, and kneeled down to help him rise. He kept shouting at the car, "Go ahead, run me over, it's the end!" I pulled at his arm, trying to get him up. "You'll get killed," I said. "Please, Mr. Weber, get up."

He seemed to recognize me. He slowly rose to his feet, his eyes suddenly frightened and seeing. I held his arm and guided him through the crowd into the store. Inside, I brought him a glass of water. He was trembling. "I'm ruined," he said. "Ruined, ruined . . ."

Mrs. Weber moaned, "We're going away. That's all, no more, we're leaving."

Meanwhile, someone had phoned the hospital, and an ambulance roared up. A young intern leaped out and pressed through the now thinning crowd of spectators into the store. "What's the matter? What happened?" He looked around. "Where's the patient?"

"I am," said Mr. Weber quietly. "I am going crazy, doctor."

The intern, startled, looked around. "He didn't feel well," I said. "I think maybe he got a sunstroke outside. He's much better now, you can see."

"You all right, Pop?" asked the intern. "How do you feel?"

Mr. Weber brushed a shaky hand across his ashen face. "I'm all right, yes."

"Lie down, take a coupla aspirins, heh?" The intern moved toward the door. With a laugh, he said, "And

don't go crazy. Too many nuts running around already."
And he departed.

There was a silence. Mrs. Weber pulled the blind down
in the front window. Mr. Weber sat in a chair, breathing
slowly, giving little groans, as though he was tired out
from running, or maybe from thinking about the big
Labor Day weekend still to come.

And I thought, Why doesn't he just go away like his
wife wants him to? Why do people stay in the same place
even though it makes them unhappy? Was it because
they couldn't leave—or were afraid to leave? I heard, at
that moment, my mother emerging from the rear house
and shouting at someone in the alley. "Get out, you can-
not peddle hats in these premises! We're not the slums.
Go to the Bowery for that!"

I rushed out and ran up to her. Surprised, laughing,
she ruffled my hair. "You're pale. Who's after you? Who's
chasing you today?"

"Mr. Weber . . . he tried to kill himself just before.
He's inside," I stammered.

With a little gasp, she lifted her hand to her mouth,
turned, and went into the store. I followed to the entrance, and stood outside. I was close enough to hear
her.

". . . A grown man like you, Mr. Weber, to do such
a thing! What's the matter with you? Is it the store rent?
We'll skip the last payment. You'll owe it to me, you'll
pay me later, next year." I heard his low sobbing, and her
voice again. "If you have no place to stay, you'll stay in
my house. Next month the season is over, I'll have empty
rooms. You're welcome to stay." She laughed, then, "Special rates for the winter! Next season will be more luck.
And where else would you find a better place to live in
all the world?"

Listening to her voice, hearing the words but not seeing her, an anger rippled through me. Why was she telling him to stay? It was wrong to tell him that. He should go somewhere else where life could be better. Here, he would find only the poor living in ugly houses, with dirt everywhere, and roaches. The games and music were just a trick to cover the ugliness.

My mother wasn't telling him any of this. Maybe she was caught in the same trap, pretending not to know. Suddenly I wanted the summer to end. I was tired of the calliope and the sound of the roller coaster and things like Mr. Weber lying down in the street to die. I wanted to forget about him. He frightened me, and my mother did too, and now I heard them laughing together inside, as if nothing happened. Maybe I'd forget it all by tomorrow. I turned to go.

Mr. Weber appeared at the door, calling to me. "Come in, boy. I'll make you a soda. Two scoops of ice cream!" I thought of running, but his eyes were very bright and brimming with tears, and I couldn't disappoint him.

∽ 15 ∾

The days arrived that told of changing weather. The sky's color hardened, the ocean added a tint of slate, and the white fleecy clouds, piling high and thick, were now scattered before the sharper winds. These winds funneled into the maze of streets to rattle the windows and send the garbage cans clattering along the sidewalk.

The house—all the houses—lost the open summery look. Doors and windows were shut by late afternoon to keep out the chill air. Striped and candy-colored awnings were rolled up and removed. Screens vanished; an occasional shutter appeared. Bath lockers and pools reduced their activities to weekends only. Slowly, as the fall advanced, merchants boarded up for the season. The pennants and pinwheels fluttered singly where they had once been massed. Kewpie dolls, their feathers thinned, were being offered at bargain prices. Popcorn was heated over and over; the whistle of the peanut machine grew weaker. Single swimmers churned in the water, but the heat-driven, heat-tormented populace had disappeared.

The boardwalk no longer drummed to the sound of shoes (millions of shoes through the summer!). A thin patter on weekends, a mere shuffle on weekdays: the movement of humanity had shifted elswhere. The nights especially revealed the change. Where the eye once saw thousands of individual bulbs blurring into a yellow haze, it now saw small islands of light in the sea of darkness. The light would continue through the winter, but would illuminate a different world. In the summer, the evening opened easily, warmly, into hours of fun that lasted until dawn. Games and roller coasters vibrated all through the night. Now the strollers rarely lingered past midnight, the rides closing soon after. Under the boardwalk, dimly lit, a world of silence and long shadows returned. Those running figures in the darkness, wild cries and guitars, had vanished: the boys and girls of summer had left their ghosts behind.

Now that school began again, I didn't have as much free time, but I liked to visit the beach after school and see how the wind combed the sand into new patterns. On this day, I watched a skinny brown ant climb a sand-ripple, hurrying to the top and tumbling down the side like a ship on a giant wave. Did he know how big the beach really was? If he knew, he'd stop walking, I thought. Or would he keep on anyway?

I looked up. Coming into sight from a distance was the bent figure of a man. He kept getting closer and larger and finally stopped nearby. He was an old man, wearing a round wool cap and a heavy-knit oversize sweater tucked into loose trousers. A weather-stained pair of salvaged military boots and a threadbare scarf completed his scarecrow attire. Across his shoulder hung a shovel and a shallow wooden tray with a wire-mesh bottom. He put the tray down, filled it with a few shovel-scoops of surface sand, raised it, and sifted the sand with a slow rotating motion. Most of the time he would find nothing on the tray but shells or stones. But there was treasure where he walked: coins, cuff links, penknives, tiepins, watches, earrings, rings, keys. I knew he would hunt this treasure all winter long, patiently crisscrossing the landscape, working most carefully under the boardwalk where in a warmer season forgotten lovers twined and grasped at one another, losing comb or coin or earring in the delirium of kisses.

I walked closer to him as he tossed and sifted the sand through the flat wire tray. He didn't seem to mind my presence. I sat and watched him the way I watched the ant. Was he going to strain the whole beach? Did he realize how big it was? It would take a thousand years! Yet he was back every year, at the end of summer. Was he the same man, or someone else? I couldn't remember. They looked alike, they looked the color of sand, as if they came up from the sand each morning and went back again at night.

I used to dig around the concrete pillars sometimes after weekends, but never found more than a couple of nickels and some hairpins. You had to have the wire tray, and also you had to be old, I thought. Maybe by being old, you knew something extra, like knowing just where to dig, and how deep.

"You find anything?" I asked the man.

He grunted. "I find, yes."

"Any money? How much?" I inquired politely.

He squinted, and paused. "Today I find a quarter and a cuff link, maybe gold. Yesterday three dimes, a nickel, some keys." He wouldn't say anymore. He kept on sifting, destroying the sand patterns while behind him new patterns emerged.

I stared out at the ocean and watched the gulls settle down on the stone jetty and go to sleep with their heads curled under their wings.

I trotted home. It was quiet in the house when I entered. My mother was strangely quiet. She closed the door and said to me, "Your grandmother is very ill. Go to her room and see her."

"Do I have to?" I didn't like that room.

"She's dying. Go in."

I shuffled to the small room where my grandmother was kept most of the time. A candle burned on the table next to her bed. She lay there, her eyes shut and clotted with a yellow watery liquid. Her skin was shriveled and tight like a mummy I remembered in a school book. I could hear her harsh irregular breathing. I moved to the bed, hesitated, leaned over her and whispered, "Grandma. I came to say hello."

Her sightless eyes blinked open. "I'm cold," she said. "Cover me."

"You're covered already, Grandma, with a big blanket."

"Liar!" she screamed. "Liar, whoever you are. You could be your mother's son or a stranger she found in the alley. I don't know you. They want me to die. All of them." She moaned. "They poisoned me."

"It's not true. You shouldn't say that."

"Your mother—who knows who your father is?—may she die before I do!" And she spat. I was stunned at her violence. She was loco, I thought. There was quiet for a moment. I asked, "Can I bring you anything?"

She turned her head away. "Where's your grandfather? I keep waiting for him. Why isn't he here? Why is he taking so long?" Her body twisted on the narrow iron bed that I had painted so many times for her. "Save me, save me," she whispered, her hand reaching out but not finding me. "Where are you? Stay with me. I'm cold."

I backed out of the room, shivering with the cold of the room and with her cold. I turned to where my mother was sitting and cried out, "We have to save her, please, Momma!"

She held me. "It's time for her to die. She wants to die. She's suffering."

"Do you want her to die?"

Her arms tightened around me. "Yes."

And then she wept.

I left the room, I had to go somewhere. I wondered how you could wish someone to die even though you loved that person. I felt a chill to my bones. Would I ever want my mother or father to die? I was terrified, and leaned against the brick wall in the alley, my breath leaping in and out of my lungs. O the answers I needed! I ran all the way to Jimmy Berkowitz, but he wasn't home. I walked back slowly, fearfully, my head lowered, watching the shadows of people on the sidewalk. I was afraid to look up at anyone.

I came back just as my father emerged from the basement, turning up the stairs with a hammer and a tray of nails. Would he tell me what I had to know? I followed him, hoping he'd see me and ask me to carry the nails, as he sometimes did. If he would only speak to me more often! I didn't care if my grandmother died as long as he was there. I didn't want him to fall into the dark spaces between the walls of the house and be lost forever. I called after him, "Poppa, I'm coming with you." He moved his head slightly. I thought he hesitated. Was he going to turn and speak?

I held my breath.